"A deep and compelling argument for living life contrary to the way the world tells you to live. In putting Christ and others first, we actually find the kingdom of God coming among us in power."

—**Mac Powell**
lead singer, THIRD DAY

. . . .

"How in the world does one advance in life by dying? The answer comes in high-definition clarity through the journey Clayton takes his readers on."

—**Tony Nolan**
evangelist, author, pastor,
and a partner in the gospel

. . . .

"*Dying to Live*…is a masterful exposition of the kind of life Jesus commands us to live by His Holy Spirit. You would do well to read it over and over again."

—**Steven Furtick**
pastor, Elevation Church, Charlotte, North Carolina
www.elevationchurch.org

. . . .

"This book contains the best of Clayton, and in it you sense the radical working of the Spirit that has characterized his ministry. I warmly recommend it!"

—**J.D. Greear**
lead pastor, the Summit Church
Durham, North Carolina

DYING TO LIVE

Abandoning Yourself to
God's Bold Paradox

CLAYTON KING

HARVEST HOUSE PUBLISHERS

EUGENE, OREGON

Cover by e210 Design, Eagan, Minnesota

DYING TO LIVE
Copyright © 2010 by Clayton King
Published by Harvest House Publishers
Eugene, Oregon 97402
www.harvesthousepublishers.com

Library of Congress Cataloging-in-Publication Data
King, Clayton, 1972-
Dying to live / Clayton King.
  p. cm.
Includes bibliographical references.
ISBN 978-0-7369-2653-9 (pbk.)
1. Christian youth—Religious life. 2. Conversion—Christianity. I. Title.
BV4531.3.K558 2010
248.8'3—dc22

2009048656

Printed in the United States of America

13 14 15 16 17 18 / VP-NI / 10 9 8 7 6

*We must invite the cross to come and
do its deadly work within us.*

A.W. Tozer

ACKNOWLEDGMENTS

I cringe when I think about all the people who deserve an acknowledgment because I will certainly leave people off this list who should be here.

My lovely wife and best friend, Charie, is my biggest fan and greatest inspiration.

My boys, Jacob and Joseph, are the joys of my life and a dream come true.

My father and mother, Joe and Jane, and my little brother, Brad, made me who I am today.

The following authors are to blame for my love of books: C.S. Lewis, J.R.R. Tolkien, Mark Twain, N.T. Wright, Ravi Zacharias, Frederick Buechner, Francis Schaeffer, John R.W. Stott, Watchman Nee, Karl Barth, Charles Spurgeon, Billy Graham, John Krakauer, Jack London, Eugene Peterson, and Ted Dekker.

Dean Parker, David Irvin, Angie Short, Sherry MacDonald, and Paul and Beth Marshall, for your kindness and generosity.

And finally, a plethora of good friends: Matt Orth, Perry Noble, Brian Burgess, Seth Stevens, Jeremy Berger, Steven Furtick, J.D. Greear, Bruce Ashford, Johnny Moore, David McKinney, Jonathan Martin, Andy Byers, M.A. Thomas, Samuel Thomas, Justin Brock, Micah Martin, Todd Gaston, Todd Still, Mac Powell, and David Nasser.

CONTENTS

Connecting with God's Big Story

I EXITED THE STAGE hot and sweaty. It had gone really well tonight. The crowd was energized and I, in turn, had plugged into their energy and preached with clarity and boldness. They were dialed in from the first word. Thousands of college students. Hungry for truth. Curious about God's will. Anxious to see their futures. Wanting to get married and be real adults. Filled with a desire to make a real difference in the world for the gospel. They hung on my every word as I talked about God, His plans, His will, His mission to redeem humanity from its fallen and broken state of misery.

Before I could make it to the back of the room to sign books at my table and meet students personally, he grabbed me by the arm. I actually saw him as I was walking down the stairs from the stage. I knew he was waiting for me and I knew it would be intense. I'd had this conversation before. Many times.

"You sounded pretty confident up there tonight. How do you know for a fact that all of what you said is true?" His question was honest enough, though it was framed in a defensive pose.

"That's a very good question," I replied, "and to be honest, the only time I'm certain I'm right is when I'm reading the Bible. Beyond that, I know I could be wrong. Is there something specific I said that you would like me to clarify? It's obvious that something has been stirred up inside of you."

He responded candidly. "It was the stuff you said about losing your life by giving it to Jesus that I don't get. How in the world do I gain life by giving it away? That sounds totally crazy to me. So I was hoping you could explain that a little more."

The last thing I wanted was to be cornered by an argumentative, know-it-all college student looking for a philosophical fight. There were dozens of people I wanted to meet, some of them brand-new converts who had just repented of their sins and been saved that very night. A crowd was already assembled at my table. I could see them from where I stood. I was tempted to blow this guy off. But he held my gaze, even though I kept glancing back at the ever-growing number of people waiting to talk to me personally.

> "I've been trying to get God to bless me and give me an easy life without giving Him any of me. That hasn't worked."

So I went straight for the jugular in hopes that if he was just an idealist who wanted to debate, I could shut him down before he got started on me. "So what is it you're really looking for right now?"

His response floored me. "I've heard tons of sermons and never really believed a word of any of them because they all seemed so shallow and fake. But tonight, I got so angry at what you were saying—all that stuff about dying to my sin and my selfishness—it just made me angrier the more you talked. But it was the first time I've ever been convinced that a sermon was true, because I was brought face-to-face with my own junk and all my anger. So I had to come meet you and tell you that. I think I finally get it. I've been trying to get God to bless me and give me an easy life without giving Him any of me. That hasn't worked.

As a matter of fact, it's made me suicidal and depressed. I want to try it the other way…I want to give Him everything and die to my past. I will try anything at this point, because my life is a wreck and I am dying to live!"

Dying to live. That is what he said.

And when I heard those words come out of his mouth, they might as well have slapped me across the face.

That is what people want. To live! They are dying for life that is filled with meaning, purpose, and a longing for something bigger and more eternal than the momentary pursuit of bigger and more stuff. And the way that life is discovered is by dying. Dying to your stubborn will, your childish pursuits, your shallow dreams, your superficial selfishness. Once that death occurs, you are resurrected to a brand-new life that is no longer about you. It isn't even yours at all. It belongs to God. And you wake up to a world filled with colors and tastes and textures and conversations and songs and laughter, a world that no longer revolves around your own petty drama but around God's bigger story of rebuilding what we all have broken.

Welcome to a new reality. One where you don't get to call the shots. One where things look odd and backward. One where you find life by giving it back to the God who gave it to you in the first place.

Welcome to *Dying to Live.*

CHAPTER 1

Laying a Foundation

*He called the crowd to him along with his disciples
and said: "If anyone would come after me, he must
deny himself and take up his cross and follow me. For
whoever wants to save his life will lose it, but whoever
loses his life for me and for the gospel will save it."*

—MARK 8:34-35

DYING TO LIVE. I know it sounds crazy. I won't try to trick you—it
is. How does someone find life by dying? This doesn't make sense and
is totally illogical, at least on the surface. If you are talking about the
actual physical act of dying, where your heart ceases to beat and your
lungs stop moving oxygen and your brain shuts down, then it's absurd
to think that life can come from that sort of death. Because when you're
dead, you're dead. That's it. You can't be "sort of" dead. It's like being
pregnant. You are. Or you're not.

But that's not what I'm talking about. That was not what Jesus was
talking about. Not at all!

In a spiritual sense, Jesus calls to us both from the Scriptures and
from His life to stand against the cultural tide, to swim upstream and
deny ourselves the indulgence of living a life just for selfish gain and
earthly pleasure. Instead, He asks us to live life in a reverse of sorts.
Where we begin to live by giving up on shallow dreams and aspirations

for safety, security, wealth, and ease and we trade those pursuits for a life of service and sacrifice and suffering all for the sake of His kingdom, His gospel, and His people. When we embrace this strange worldview, we die to our selfishness and sin and awaken to the life that only God can breathe into our nostrils. As with the first man, Adam, the wind from God's mouth inhabits our dry, lifeless dust and we take on flesh and bone and blood, and we live!

When we fully embrace a life lived in reverse, as it were, we are acting like Jesus acted. We are loving like Jesus loved. We are giving like Jesus gave. We are, indeed, *following* Jesus when we die to live. Billy Graham says it this way:

> He [Christ] came to reveal God to man. He it is who told us that God loves us and is interested in our lives. He it is who told us of the mercy and long-suffering and grace of God. He it is who promised everlasting life. But more than that, Jesus partook of flesh and blood in order that He might die (Hebrews 2:14). He was manifested to take away our sins (1 John 3:5). The very purpose of Christ's coming into the world was that He might offer up His life as a sacrifice for the sins of me. He came to die.[1]

Where We're Going

To drive the idea that we find life in Christ by dying to sin and self-ishness, I will employ a variety of tools: personal stories, parable-like incidents, word pictures, historical illustrations, and honest, as well as humorous, anecdotes and insights from life and Scripture.

And, that is really what this book is all about: Exploring the paradoxical notion that life is really found by embracing a sort of death. But it is a good death, if death can indeed ever be good. And we can live this way because Jesus came to die, and did die, and rose from death never to die again. We find life by losing our rights, our cravings, our wants, and our obsessions. We embrace death to all the things that would eventually kill you and me anyway:

- death to a life wasted on the pursuit of personal pleasures that never last more than a few moments

- death to decades of attempting to please people who don't know me or love me

- death to the nightmarish existence of working jobs just for things like houses, cars, vacations, and retirement accounts

- death to a life filled with anxiety and stress over finances and retirement that leads to heart disease that would kill me in my late forties

- death to the obsession with having more things, which demands I work more and stay home less and eventually get divorced

- death to a fast-paced lifestyle that cripples all family relationships and leads to an affair, which costs me everything of real value

- death to childish envy and jealousy that arises when friends and colleagues live a lifestyle better than mine

And while work and homes and investments and retirement accounts are by no means evil, when I begin to place my wholehearted devotion on these pursuits and the pleasure and safety I feel when I achieve them, then I replace total trust in God with temporary trust in my accomplishments. Jesus wants to kill that in me before it kills me. That is how I awaken to His life. Real life. A life that is not tethered to the false securities and fake promises our world gives to me.

Eventually, I will die. So will you. (Do not fear. This is not a morbid book on death. So keep reading.) And if I live for Him, isn't dying for Him the natural way to leave this world, whether I die as a martyr on the mission field or as an old man in a hospital bed?

Plain and simple, I am not concerned with cute stories or clever insights that encourage and inspire you, nor will I attempt to manipulate your emotions by telling story after story of people who loved God more than you do and sacrificed more for God than you have. Guilt is a terrible motivational tool that never lasts more than a few minutes.

I am more compelled to deal with a deeper heart issue—an issue that followers of Jesus Christ must, at some point, come face-to-face with. The question is asked simply but answered with greater difficulty.

Am I really alive right now beyond having a pulse? If so, what am I really living for?

CHAPTER 2

What Would I Die For?

IT SOUNDS EPIC. Like the stuff of a great movie plot. The kind where the hero or heroine abandons all earthly attachments for a greater cause, sacrificing life and limb and eventually, as Jon Bon Jovi sang, going down in a blaze of glory. These kinds of stories, books, and movies have many fans and make lots of money. They tap into an innate human admiration for those who possess a willingness to give up their lives for some higher virtue or cause. Or put another way, we connect emotionally to heroes who are willing to die in order to live or in order for others to live through their sacrifice.

Two epic Hollywood blockbusters have made hundreds of millions of dollars off of just such an idea in my lifetime. I love them both. I own them both. And when either comes on television, I will drop everything to watch. I get sucked in, like the tractor beam on the Death Star pulling in Han Solo and the *Millennium Falcon*.

It was the Spaniard Maximus, who fought his way from the grimy outposts of the Roman Empire, was taken as a slave, and was forced to fight for his life in *Gladiator,* who caught the attention of so many

Americans. He was noble and firm and honorable. His family was killed brutally and he was eventually taken off to Rome, where he was killed by the villain in the Roman Coliseum and carried off to his grave on the shoulders of admiring men, some of whom were still loyal to this former Roman general. The movie was a runaway hit, made buckets of cash, and made Russell Crowe into a Hollywood A-list actor. In my opinion, he can never top his performance. It was the way the Gladiator lived that so inspired both fans and critics. It was the way he died that made him an unforgettable character.

But it was the fiery and fierce Scottish rogue William Wallace that, at least for my generation, set the standard for sacrifice, bravery, and courage. Mel Gibson, in the movie *Braveheart*, showed many a young American male exactly how to die, because he knew what he was living for. He was living for Scotland, for love, for revenge, for freedom! He died for those ideals, at least in the movie, but his legend lives on, far greater and more enduring because he gave his life for others.

> If my life is devoted to something... that will outlive me and outlast my existence, then the years I spend on earth are not spent making a name or a place for me.

In the closing scene of the movie, which I dare any man to watch emotionless, Wallace faces certain death with defiance and fearlessness. He has nothing left to live for because he has already given his all for his people, his kith and kin. And he leaves an example for all other Scotsmen to remember, and to emulate. Given a pain-numbing substance by his French lover just before his execution, he spits it out upon her departure. He doesn't desire numbness. He wants to feel all the suffering that awaits him. Given the chance to recant and beg for mercy in exchange for a quick and painless death, he opts for disembowelment. And in one of the most epic scenes in motion-picture history, Wallace screams at the top of his lungs, as they fill with his last breath, the very thing he had fought for. FREEDOM!

His death would have been lackluster if we had not seen how he had lived on the big screen before he died.

This is how it is with Jesus. His death alone would mean nothing were it not for how He lived. It was in His living that He gave His death, and eventually His resurrection, the traction to stick in people's hearts.

This is how it is with us. We die like we live, and we must live in such a deliberate way as to assure that when we do die, no matter the cause or context, we as followers of Jesus will leave this life, not basking in our own glory of accomplishments and accolades, but in anticipation of His glory. We find meaning and purpose when we live for something bigger and greater than us.

If my little insignificant 75-year existence on earth is the grand sum of all things, then my life will be filled with the impossible stress of trying harder and harder to make my small life count for something before I die. But if my life is devoted to something much bigger, something that will outlive me and outlast my existence, then the years I spend on earth are not spent on making a name or a place for me, but for the greater mission of helping build a kingdom that will last for eternity. I want to be a part of that kingdom. I am dying to live like that.

I AM DYING TO LIVE LIKE THAT!

The Right Question

Scenes such as those from *Gladiator* and *Braveheart* are seared into the American collective subconscious. So much so that when we think of dying for someone or something (as opposed to dying of old age or a disease like cancer or a heart attack), we picture ourselves as the epic hero figure: bloodied, broken, defiant, resolute, and unwavering. Sitting in a movie theater, I would much prefer to die like one of the American GI's valiantly storming the cliffs of Normandy in *Saving Private Ryan* or like Mel Gibson, a Scottish firebrand unafraid of death and the devil.

The real truth is different, however, for the majority of humans. We will all, mostly, die of natural causes. A few of us will get hit by a bus, struck by lightning, or bitten by a poisonous snake or tick. Others will die in their sleep, in their automobile, or in an airplane crash. But with the exception of the occasional mad-cow-disease death, the more common fare will be our undoing. Diabetes. Kidney failure. Lung cancer. Stroke. Our bodies will age and

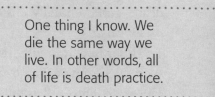

One thing I know. We die the same way we live. In other words, all of life is death practice.

wear out in time. They will gradually cease to function efficiently and properly until, like my own father has told me, we actually look forward to death.

Sounds morbid, I know. But I'm trying to be realistic here. Death is batting a thousand (in baseball terms), with one glaring exception. Jesus cheated death. But He still died before His resurrection. And so will I. And you will too. Eventually. It is coming and it will take us down. In light of this melancholy realization, there is a wrong question to ask and a right question to ask.

- The wrong question: How will I die?
- The right question: How will I live until I die?

And that is indeed the issue to deal with while we still have life to live ahead of us. How will I live right now? And what will I live for before death comes knocking?

One thing I know. We die the same way we live. In other words, all of life is death practice.

Johnny Hunt, the pastor of a large church in the Atlanta area, told a story once that made an impression on me. When he was young in the ministry, an older gentleman took him under his wing, befriended him, and became a supporter and mentor. Before the church had reached its current size and before Dr. Hunt was able to draw a salary from his church, this older man had made it a habit to always slip the pastor some cash in his hand as they were leaving one another's company. Primitive Baptists, who never paid their pastors a salary, would instead pay them with these "hundred-dollar handshakes." Dr. Hunt said that almost every time they were together, this man would discreetly hand him some bills.

The man eventually fell ill and was on his deathbed. Dr. Hunt went to visit him in the hospital. As he entered the room, the older man saw Dr. Hunt and instinctively reached for his wallet in his back pocket. It had been his practice in life. He was still practicing it upon his death.

We die in the same manner in which we live. By the time of our death, it's too late to change anything. Our death will be a reflection of our life. If we live only for ourselves, we lose everything once we draw our last breath. If we live for the kingdom and the gospel and the glory of Christ, we gain everything—we live before we die, and we really live after death!

Embracing a Paradox

My hope in this endeavor, this book I have labored on, which you now hold in your hands, is that you live the remainder of your days with eternity in mind. I hope you will consider your death and your eternity *before* you go any further in life. Ask yourself, *Is this how I want to invest the rest of my time, work, and efforts in this world?* We only get one shot at life on Planet Earth. There are no do-overs. I want to make this round count. I know you do as well. So let's live our life with the end in view and make it count for something bigger and more important than ourselves.

How do we do this? That's the question, isn't it? How do we convert our thinking from self-preservation and pride to service, humility, and wholehearted devotion to God and others?

We do it by embracing the often confusing and always convicting paradox of Jesus Christ. The God who became a man. The Deity who died and arose from death. The Master who washed people's dirty feet. The Savior who submitted to service. We have gained life from His death, and now we participate daily in living out that life by continually dying to all things that would exalt self and sin and pride. It doesn't make sense to the natural, superficial individual that we would do things backward and actually find peace and purpose in life by losing our own rights to call the shots and steer the course, but that is exactly what Jesus commands us to do. It seems odd. It is. So are most aspects of the Christian life. And that is the point Jesus drives home when He claims we can find real life by losing it—by turning it over to Him.

> Lord, high and holy, meek and lowly,
>> Thou hast brought me to the valley of vision,
>> Where I live in the depths but see in the heights;
>> Hemmed in by mountains of sin I behold thy glory.
> Let me learn by paradox
>> That the way down is the way up,
>> That to be low is to be high,
>> That the broken heart is the healed heart,
>> That the contrite spirit is the rejoicing spirit,
>> That the repenting soul is the victorious soul,
>> That to have nothing is to possess all,
>> That to bear the cross is to wear the crown,
>> That to give is to receive, that the valley is the place of vision
> Lord, in the daytime stars can be seen from deepest wells,
>> And the deeper the wells the brighter thy stars shine:
>> Let me find thy light in my darkness,
>>> Thy life in my death,
>>> Thy joy in my sorrow,
>>> Thy grace in my sin,
>>> Thy riches in my poverty,
>>> Thy glory in my valley.[2]
>
> —from The Valley of Vision

CHAPTER 3

Thomas—A Man of Contradictions

BESIDES THE COLLEGE STUDENT who used the phrase *dying to live,* God used Thomas, one of the twelve disciples, as a biblical catalyst for the big idea of this book: that Jesus is worth living and dying for, and it is only in dying to ourselves that we find life in Jesus. You might imagine that if I were picking biblical characters to inspire devotion and sacrifice, Thomas would be toward the bottom of the list. Right above other stellar stalwarts of faith like Samson, Barabbas, and Judas.

However, when I picture what Thomas must have been like, I see him as a complex, honest, and bold man. Interestingly, when I think of him, my mind automatically goes to an old friend from my younger days in ministry. His name was Mick. I picture him when I think of Thomas. He was outspoken, said exactly what was on his mind, and never left any room for interpretation about what he meant to say.

When Mick became a Christian, he left a life of drugs and alcohol abuse behind and began pursuing Jesus with the same energy and vitality with which he had pursued all the sinful and destructive things before conversion. We would be at church or at a Bible study, and he would blurt out the most inappropriate questions and comments! He was just downright embarrassing. But he didn't know any better because he was a new believer. Once, in regard to the Trinity, he said,

"There is no way that can be true. It just doesn't make sense that God exists in three Persons. Even God can't do that." Sound familiar? I could hear Thomas saying this.

But Mick also possessed an immediate willingness to do anything for the gospel. All you had to do was ask him and he would set up chairs, drive his car to pick up supplies, or witness to the most hardcore atheist or drug dealer around. Once he stood toe to toe with an angry and belligerent drug dealer on one of our Friday night witnessing excursions. I was afraid to even get close to the guy for fear he might do me bodily harm, but my friend never hesitated and within a few moments, he was sharing the gospel with one of the most feared street thugs in our region. He never backed down even though he didn't understand everything there was to know about following Christ.

Mick's honest doubts did not dampen his desire to give all he had to Jesus. This is how I picture Thomas.

❦

Thomas is known almost universally as a doubter. His lack of faith and the famous statement, "Unless I can thrust my hands into the scars on his hands and feet and side, I will not believe that Jesus is alive," gained him the label "Doubting Thomas." That's too bad for him. He got branded. (I know how it is to get stuck with a nickname you hate even if you earned it. My second-grade teacher called me "mouth of the South"; and you can imagine the fun my classmates had with that one, especially after the teacher gave them the idea and a license to use it.) That is about all the average Christian knows about Thomas. He doubted the risen Lord.

But that's not all there is to this disciple. Since so little is revealed about him in Scripture, relatively little has been written about him from a scholarly or a devotional perspective. The Gospels just don't give us much to go on when it comes to Thomas. He is mentioned only a handful of times in a few places. We know he had a twin, either

a brother or a sister, because he was called
"Didymus" or twin. This
was simply a way of dis-
tinguishing him from
the other Thomases of
his day, like when two
boys in the same class

> If the gospel writers had just given us a wee bit more in the way of information about Thomas...we could be more assured of this disciple and what he was really made of.

with the same first name will go by the first letter of their last name, for instance, Scott C. and Scott G.

Thomas was a Jew with evident skepticism. This was probably his personality. Some people are just born that way. It has even been suggested that Thomas was plagued with a sense of melancholy throughout life, much like what many historians have said about Abraham Lincoln. But honestly, who really knows? If the Gospel writers had just given us a wee bit more in the way of information about Thomas, stories about him, facts or events—anything—we could be more assured of this disciple and what he was really made of.

Evidently that was not God's intent. Thomas gets a scattered few mentions in the Bible. And that's it.

The few times he is mentioned, he is named in the list of disciples; he is demanding evidence that the disciples have indeed seen the real Jesus after the crucifixion on Golgotha; he is making an odd and bold statement—a statement in the context of going with Jesus into a hostile territory, a dangerous area where death seemed a great possibility if not a certainty.

It is this final time I mention, the brief appearance by Thomas in John 11 and his assertion he wanted to be with Jesus, that arrested my heart and soul the first time I read it. And it was indeed this statement by "Doubting Thomas" that sparked in me the vision for this book and opened my eyes to the words of Christ: that we find life by losing it. Perhaps Thomas had heard those paradoxical words of Jesus around campfires as they traveled throughout the Judean countryside, or maybe he had heard Jesus say them as He preached to crowds along the way. It seems like Thomas was listening, like he had sunk his teeth into the words of Christ and they had settled into his heart. In case you have forgotten them, here they are again. Straight from the mouth of the incarnate Son of God.

> *If anyone would come after me, he must deny himself and take up his cross and follow me. For whoever wants to save his life will lose it, but whoever loses his life for me will find it* (Matthew 16:24).

Jesus had made some enemies by the time we see Him in John 11. They had already tried to kill Him, as a matter of fact. Read it for yourself.

> *Again the Jews picked up stones to stone him, but Jesus said to them, "I have shown you many great miracles from the Father. For which of these do you stone me?"*
> *"We are not stoning you for any of these," replied the Jews, "but for blasphemy, because you, a mere man, claim to be God"* (John 10:31-33).

The one word that really sticks out in these verses is the word "again." Again? How many times had they tried to kill Jesus? This was not the first time the Jewish leadership had gotten stirred up enough to try and execute Jesus on the spot, without so much as a trial!

Jesus really knew how to rile them up, for sure. Yet in some way, He eluded them.

> *Again they tried to seize him, but he escaped their grasp* (John 10:39).

So somehow Jesus makes it out with His life intact. The disciples were there with Him when this attempt on His life took place and were certainly glad to be standing in safer territory. They weren't booking vacations in that region ever again.

Right on the heels of this murder attempt, Jesus takes His disciples across the Jordan River, where many people believed in Him. While there, He gets word from the town of Bethany that a very good friend of His lies sick and suffering. This friend is Lazarus. Jesus was not only an intimate friend of His, but was also close to his sisters, Mary and Martha. (The New Testament actually gives a more prominent role to these three siblings than to Thomas.) It is evident that Jesus cared deeply for this family. He had been with them in their home often. They had prepared meals for Him, and there is no telling what the Bible leaves unrevealed about their friendship. Suffice it to say, He loved them. Especially Lazarus.

When the message is delivered, there is a sense of urgency, based on the historical and cultural context. In the first century, when someone fell ill, there were no doctors, emergency rooms, or pharmacies to appeal to for help. The smallest sickness could lead to quick death. People died of common and curable ailments like toothaches, skin infections, and cuts on their feet. So when the sisters send word to Jesus that Lazarus is sick, the translation is simple.

"HELP! Lazarus is going to die if You don't get to Bethany ASAP and heal him. Hurry up!"

But instead of mobilizing the men and making tracks to Judea, Jesus decides to stay put for another couple of days. Of course, He does this on purpose so that Mary, Martha, the community there in Bethany, and Lazarus himself, would realize that He is not just some prophet who has healing powers. He is actually God, because He can raise the dead. His delay is intentional. He intends to give them a new revelation of who He is as His power and authority over death are revealed.

When Jesus does finally decide the time is right to pay Lazarus (now dead) and his sisters a visit, the disciples are utterly perplexed. What good is it to go visit a dead man, other than to pay your respects? But the real issue revolves around their safety, not Lazarus. For them, a trip toward Lazarus' corpse in the town of Bethany means putting themselves in harm's way, "getting sideways" (as the old expression goes) with some ill-tempered religious folk who had no shortage of ill-will toward Jesus and any who kept company with Him.

> *Jesus loved Martha and her sister and Lazarus. Yet when he heard that Lazarus was sick, he stayed where he was two more days. Then he said to his disciples, "Let us go back to Judea." "But Rabbi," they said, "a short while ago the Jews tried to stone you, and yet you are going back there?"* (John 11:5-8).

The bottom line: They hate Jesus in the very area the disciples are about to walk into, and the religious folk attempted to murder Him the last time He visited. And the disciples know it. Since they are with Jesus, they will be found guilty by association. If another attempt is made to kill Jesus, they may get caught in the crossfire. None of them are volunteering for the journey.

So when Jesus decides to go back there to see dead Lazarus, the disciples freak out. They were relieved when He turned down the request two days earlier. Now He changes His mind and imperils each of them in His crazy death wish. If He goes back there, they will kill Him. If they *all* go back there, they will kill them *all*. So when He tries to rally the boys, the response is predictable.

> *The last time you were in Judea, the Jews tried to kill you there.*

Translation: "We don't want to go because we don't want to die. Don't press Your luck, Lord. You made it out alive once—be thankful for it and avoid confrontation. And anyway, we have all left our jobs and communities and families to follow You as our Rabbi, so if You die, what will we do? We would rather not have to return to our previous jobs. It would embarrass us to admit that we followed a failure for three years. Stay here where it's safe. Let's keep things predictable, manageable, free of drama and death."

They had not yet found life because they had not yet lost it. Not in their hearts.

Just as with us, their mission was self-preservation. They wanted the easiest route with the fewest complications. They did not want to be inconvenienced. They were safe and sound two days away from the hotheads who hated their Rabbi so vehemently, and they were fine hanging out there indefinitely. But Jesus treated them like He treats us. He would not let them sit still and grow apathetic. He intended to lead them into dangerous territory, both in the short term and in the long run. He wanted to go right into the thick of things, and He wanted them to be by His side.

Jesus has not changed. He still calls every disciple, every Christian, whether American or Chinese, African or Latino, to go where they would not choose to go. He compels us to launch into deeper and scarier waters. Waters we have never navigated before. Waters that cause us to feel fear, trepidation, and panic. He leads us into places that force us to trust Him.

> It is better to die with Jesus than to live without Him. This is the phrase that now haunts my thoughts, my dreams, my daily routine.

The chorus of voices was attempting to get Jesus to think about things logically. The consensus was simply that going in that direction, toward Bethany, was a bad idea because of all the trouble that awaited them, namely death.

But there was one lone voice that spoke in dissent from the urging of the disciples.

It was Thomas.

Then Thomas (called Didymus) said to the rest of the disciples, "Let us also go, that we may die with him" (John 11:16).

Did you hear that? Go read it again. Listen to it with your heart, not just your head. The boys want to stay, but Thomas wants to go. Go where?

Anywhere Jesus goes. Even to die with Him.

Thomas said that. Of all people. Doubting Thomas.

"Let us also go, that we may die with him." A simple phrase that communicates a harsh realization. It is better to die with Jesus than to live without Him. This is the phrase that now haunts my thoughts, my dreams, my daily routine. *Why am I alive? That I may die with Him.* This is how I find life, and the very reason so many people today don't have life despite all the things they have filled their lives with. You aren't really alive until you have seen what Thomas saw and understood what Thomas knew. Jesus is life! Therefore, life apart from knowing Christ is simply existence, not really living. Not real life. Until a person sees Jesus in His beauty and glory, they just exist until death takes them. Once we recognize Him as Lord and Savior, we are dying to live, for Him and His gospel and His kingdom.

There are times, almost daily, when I forget that Jesus is my life and I revert to an old way of thinking, before I met Christ, before I died to my sins in repentance, when I was the center of the universe and the most important thing to myself. Like every other human on earth, I tend to think the infinite cosmos revolves around me. All my decisions are made based on what will benefit me, what is best for me, what is most convenient for me, what will cause me the least amount of stress and anxiety, and how I can get a bigger piece of the American dream for myself.

Yet I am constantly confronted with the ugly truth that my life now belongs to Another and I am no longer my own. It is now my joy and duty to serve Christ and others and in doing so, bring glory to God and joy to others. Ownership has changed hands. I am not my own anymore.

Do you not know that your body is a temple of the Holy Spirit,
who is in you, whom you have received from God? You are not

*your own; you were bought at a price. Therefore honor God
with your body* (1 Corinthians 6:19-20).

As offensive as this concept is, as much as it flies in the face of our
sense of rugged, independent individualism, the brutal truth is simple.
Jesus ransomed me, or bought me, out of slavery to sin and my own
selfishness. He redeemed me and now He calls the shots. And daily I,
and all of His followers, have opportunities in abundance to live out
the new life we have been given by dying to the old way of life.

- When I am too tired to drive to the airport for one more
  preaching event. I do it by His grace in spite of my fatigue.

- When my back aches from three consecutive nights in hotel
  beds and I have one more night to be away from my family.
  All because I am called to preach the gospel.

- When my wife is sick and I don't feel like putting the boys
  to bed. I tuck them in because I belong to Christ now and
  they belong to Him, too.

- When my father needs me to sit with him all night after
  triple-bypass surgery and I have a deadline to meet for a
  writing project. I know what takes priority.

- When a brother in Christ is financially broke due to an un-
  controllable circumstance and I can help him out, but it
  means saying no to something I really wanted for myself. I
  must write the check.

- When my son begs me to read him a book but I need to get
  one more e-mail sent. The computer can wait.

- When I could fudge just a little bit on my monthly expense
  report, but that small compromise would lead to eventual
  destruction. I must tell the truth.

I slip back into the same mind-set the disciples had when Jesus
wanted to deliberately lead them into deadly and dangerous territory.
I want what is easiest, safest, and most convenient. But then the Holy

Spirit speaks to me, as I am sure He does to you, and reminds me that my life is not my own anymore. I am compelled by a greater calling and a greater mission than my own self-preservation.

My life is now bound up in this strange paradox. I can find life only by embracing death: the eventual death of my body and the immediate death of my sinful, selfish nature. A willingness, an eagerness, to die with Jesus. And to eternally live with Jesus. This is the great mystery of the gospel, that in following Jesus I must die to myself and in doing so be made truly alive! I die in order to live. Dead to sin. Dead to selfishness. Dead to greedy ambition. Alive to Christ. Alive because of Christ.

CHAPTER 4

Finding Life by Finding Something to Die For

I have been crucified with Christ and I no longer live, but Christ lives in me. The life I live in the body, I live by faith in the Son of God, who loved me and gave himself for me.

—GALATIANS 2:20

OF THE 12 MEN who followed Christ, it was Thomas who tapped into sheer, perfect revelation. He got it!

He was the first disciple, as I see it, to really understand what Jesus was all about and who Jesus really was. When the rest are thinking of saving life and limb, Thomas blurts out something so absurd, so odd, that it seems surreal.

In essence, he says he has found the very thing he was born for in Jesus, and life without Jesus would be unthinkable. He was willing to die in order to live.

Imagine with me for just a moment what the Gospel writer didn't tell us, but what Thomas may have said to the disciples when they looked at him like he was crazy for suggesting they all go to their deaths with Jesus. It may have sounded like this:

"Boys, we have been following this man for a long time. We have heard His teachings and seen what He is capable of doing. I am certain

He is the anointed one, the Messiah, promised from the prophets of old, come to set God's people free. I am following Him wherever He leads. And if He goes to Judea, I am going with Him. We all need to go with Him. He is our Rabbi, our master, and we are His disciples. If the Jews kill Him there, then I want to die by His side. I want to be with Him where He leads and where He goes. I cannot think of letting Him go alone or staying behind. I will die with Him! We all should be willing to die with Him. So let's quit talking. Let's get moving."

It's all but impossible to explain this kind of deep devotion to someone. It can only be understood by experiencing it, by embracing it, and by being transformed spiritually as a result. Dying to live is easier caught than taught. But I still try to tell people about it.

🕆

I tried to explain this life perspective once to a gentleman on an airplane and, to be frank, he just did not get it. At all. I shouldn't be surprised, though, especially since the entire idea of dying to live is held in utter contempt in a shallow and superficial culture that esteems greed and possessions instead of sacrifice and humility.

> "So is there anything in life that you would be willing to die for? Without hesitating?"

The conversation began easily enough. Two men being cordial. Sitting side by side on an airplane. The obligatory questions when striking up a conversation on an airplane go as follows:

So where are you heading today?
How long will you be there?
What kind of work do you do?
Where is your home?

With these four essential questions, I can get just about anyone to open up. The expectation is that once I have asked these questions, they will immediately return the favor and ask me what I do for a living. When I tell them I am a minister, there is no predicting how they will respond. I've been hugged, yelled at, cursed, and asked, "Why would you want to do that?" Yeah, it's always an adventure.

In the conversation I'm recounting, I had gotten deep enough with the gentleman beside me that I decided to throw a curve ball at him. Since I wanted to share the gospel with him anyway, I felt confident I would have to shake things up a bit to get his attention, since he was a smug and self-confident professional who seemed sure of himself and without the need for God at all. You should have seen the look on his face when, after he'd told me of all his great accomplishments, accumulations, and aspirations, I sideswiped him with this little question.

"So is there anything in life you would be willing to die for? Without hesitating? On the spot, immediately, is there anything you would lay down your life for this very moment?"

He was dumbfounded.

"Well, that is a strange question. I suppose, well, uh, I need to think about that."

He took a second and responded, "I think I would die for my kids, like, if someone had them tied up with a gun to their head and said they would kill them or me, I would like to think I would take the bullet for them. But I'm not sure."

I said, "That is admirable of you. I think any good father would do that under those circumstances." I stopped. I wanted to let the conversation breathe, give it some space. Let him ask me the next question. I knew he would.

In spiritual conversations, I have learned to ask leading questions, those that invite the other person to be curious, to ask certain things that go deeper to the heart. The average person is much more willing to listen and engage when they feel that a respectful invitation has been extended to them versus that they're being assaulted by a religious expert who knows everything there is to know about God and how to correct everyone else where they are misguided. When I employed this conviction with the guy to my left he was more than willing to talk.

"So what about you?" he countered. "Is there anything you would die for, right now, if you had the chance?" His question to me was my open door.

"Well, I am not some kind of epic hero, and I have never served in the military or anything. But to be honest with you, yes, there is one thing. As a matter of fact, the strange irony is, I have already done it. I have already died, and the life I am now living, I am living as a result of my first death."

He thought I was a lunatic. But he couldn't let an odd statement like that go unchallenged.

"What in the world are you talking about?"

I prayed that God would give him understanding when I responded.

And for the next ten minutes, I described to him, as best I knew how, the paradox of following Jesus and finding life by giving it away. That when I died to my sin and selfishness by the power of the gospel, I became alive in a much more real way. And because I had experienced the death of my old self, my new self was really alive, like hyper-alive. I was now willing to die for the gospel, but also was willing, and indeed was literally, living for the gospel. And that every day of living for Christ was allowing me to become "deader and deader" to the way I used to be before I was saved from my sins.

I wish I could give you a good report and tell you he was overcome with conviction and gave his life to Jesus right there on the spot. But alas, it didn't turn out that way. Instead, though, he said something just as compelling.

"Wow. I have never thought about it that way. You have really given me something to consider. I will have to really think about that some more, because I am certainly not at that place in life."

His candor was refreshing even though I was slightly disappointed that the conversation ended at that point (though I pray God is still speaking to him). His response also makes the point that living this radical life of discipleship demands some serious consideration, and not everyone is automatically attracted to it. In other words, if you think it is going to be easy, then you have missed the point entirely. It is difficult. It requires sacrifice, doing without, putting something besides you into the central place of importance. Following Jesus is the most difficult endeavor you will ever embark on. Because He is leading, not you. And the places He intends to take us cause severe discomfort and inconvenience.

I feel it's important for a follower of Jesus to be disciplined in the aspects of the Christian life we focus on, both in our own spiritual growth and as we act as witnesses to the gospel. It would have been much easier to talk to the man on the airplane about the love and mercy and grace of Christ in such a way as to give him an impression that converting to faith in Jesus would mean a much easier future with more predictable outcomes, where all the bills would be paid on time and nobody ever got sick or died.

But being a witness to the gospel means telling the truth, both to ourselves and those we share it with. The truth is that Jesus lays a hard claim on us and makes some heavy demands that require sacrifice on our part. The life of a disciple is not always Sunday-morning worship with choirs and choruses. It's filled with sorrow and joy, celebration and lament, losses and gains, all for the sake of knowing Christ and being His own possession. I felt it was important to share this candidly with the man beside me on the plane, and I feel the same urgency to share it with you.

Dying to live is not trendy, sexy, or cool. But it's the only way to gain life, the only way to know Jesus, the only way to be free from the trap of living for yourself and dying hopeless.

So give yourself completely to God. Let Him kill the things in you that would ultimately destroy you. Gain life by giving it away.

You and I can go through this process only if God does it in us; but God can do it only if He becomes man. Our attempts at this dying will succeed only if we men share in God's dying, just as our thinking can succeed only because it is a drop out of the ocean of His intelligence: but we cannot share God's dying unless God dies: and He cannot die except by being a man. That is the sense in which He pays our debt, and suffers for us what He Himself need not suffer at all.[3]

CHAPTER 5

Dying to Position and Authority

THE STRANGE IRONY of the world that Jesus was born into is simply seen by one fact. The religious professionals, who of all people should have recognized the Messiah (after all, they had studied and memorized the prophets of ancient Judaism that had spoken of His arrival), totally missed Him. As a matter of fact, they didn't just miss Him. They antagonized Him. They tortured Him. They murdered Him. He turned their neatly ordered world upside down and they hated Him for it. They forced a yoke of slavery on the people and He came to set them free.

What made Jesus so odd, so aggravating, and so unique?

It was His unmistakable sense of purpose that set Him apart and set His enemies on the warpath. Jesus came to die. Period. His entire existence as a man was defined by this sense of destiny. His opponents existed to rule over people. Therefore they conducted themselves and their business with a sense of pride and smug arrogance, assuming a position of unquestioned authority over their subjects. One of the prayers the Pharisees commonly prayed in public, on street corners in front of large crowds, went like this: "God, I thank You that I am not a woman, a sinner, or a Gentile dog." Don't you just feel the self-love?

Jesus conducted Himself in a completely different manner because He was here on a completely different mission. He came to die so we might live. His life was characterized by a sense of humility and service, diametrically opposed to the attitude of the Pharisees and religious leaders. No wonder they hated Christ so vehemently. He was everything they were not. They wanted to rule. He came to serve. They existed to live a life of ease. He came to die. It is hard to imagine Jesus vaunting His superiority or standing in public praying to be heard or posturing to be seen.

The Pharisees took pride in their position. Jesus lowered Himself by laying down His life, by dying as a sacrifice in our place, and giving us life through His death and resurrection.

He died to live.

One of the men who has had the greatest influence over my life and ministry is a pastor in South Carolina named Ronnie. He is a pretty good preacher (most Sundays he would say he is about average), but he is a fantastic pastor. He preaches funerals and has seen thousands of people respond to the gospel at funerals and graveside services. He spends half the week visiting the sick, shut-ins, and anyone in the hospital. He is always there for people, especially when they are broken and hurting. If you were to meet him, the one characteristic about Ronnie that would stick with you would be his humility. You would never know that before he met Christ, he was a man of great means, great wealth, and authority.

> He lost all his accomplishments when he surrendered his life to Christ, and he eventually became a pastor. But it was death that brought about that transformation.

He died to his position and authority one afternoon on the side of the road. Though he had wealth and possessions and people taking orders from him, the moment that changed everything for him was the death of his brother. A tragic motorcycle accident occurred, and he found himself holding his dying brother in his arms in a ditch on the side of the highway. As his brother drew his last breath, Ronnie looked up to heaven and cried out to God for help. God helped him, but not in the way he expected. He did not spare his brother but spared Ronnie; instead of saving his brother from dying, He saved Ronnie from dying by rescuing him from his own pompous pursuits of pleasure and worldly prominence. These things would have lasted for only a season, but salvation is eternal.

Ronnie gave his life to Christ right there in that ditch, the body of his brother still warm in his arms. He lost all his accomplishments when he surrendered his life to Christ, and he eventually became a pastor. But it was death that brought about that transformation. Death brought life. Did God kill his brother? you may ask. No, but He used that tragedy to bring a man to his knees, to the end of himself, and to faith. When Ronnie tells that story now at funerals, not a dry eye remains.

Pride of Position

God will use whatever it takes to break us of our pride and show us that our accomplishments, accolades, and positions are worthless without His grace. He used a virgin-born Jewish boy who would eventually be slaughtered on a filthy Roman cross to make this point to an arrogant religious establishment that took great pride in being seen, heard, known, and respected.

The Jewish religious hierarchy of the first century was not willing, at all, to lose their lives for the people they were given stewardship over. They expected the sheep to care for the shepherds. Jesus instead came as a real shepherd intent on caring for the sheep and protecting them from the wolves—wolves that were, ironically, dressed in the finest religious robes, with the Law of God hanging around their necks and falling off their lips. He assumed a position of humility and service. Though He was fully God, He made Himself last and least.

We are expected to follow suit. In essence, we die daily to all that is within us that wants to rise up and rule over others. In this daily dying, we become more alive to what it means to be Christian.

Jesus' humility was a characteristic of God Himself, fleshed out in human skin. Here, the prophet Isaiah immediately comes to mind. Nearly 700 years before the virgin-born baby entered a Bethlehem barn, Isaiah spoke of the coming Messiah in surprising terms. The anointed one would look surprisingly normal. His physical appearance would not draw the attention of the crowd as one would expect. In symbolism strikingly similar to the story of King David, the Messiah would not take our breath away with His good looks.

God had done this consistently in His dealings with His people. He was known to pick the lowest and then elevate them to the position of greatest importance. In 2 Samuel, the prophet Samuel goes to the house of Jesse to anoint a new king over the nation of Israel. The proud father parades his sons across the stage, certain that the visible good looks and accomplishments of the older sons will impress the reluctant prophet. But in true upside-down fashion, God rejects the obvious first-round draft picks and goes straight to the junior varsity for His king. He chose the youngest of all the brothers. He picked the runt of the litter. The king He chose was working a day's journey away tending sheep, a job reserved for the youngest son, or hired hands, or the lowest servants.

God's paradox is seen in the fact that the most humble of the family was His handpicked king. Just like God choosing a persecutor of Christians to be the greatest evangelist in history. Just like God choosing to come to earth as a wee baby in a barn. Humility is one of His favorite traits.

We get a snapshot of the humility of Christ in that amazing part of Paul's letter to his friends in the Philippian church.

> *Your attitude should be the same as that of Christ Jesus: Who, being in very nature God, did not consider equality with God something to be grasped, but made himself nothing, taking the*

*very nature of a servant, being made in human likeness. And
being found in appearance as a man, he humbled himself and
became obedient to death—even death on a cross! Therefore
God exalted him to the highest place and gave him the name
that is above every name, that at the name of Jesus every knee
should bow, in heaven and on earth and under the earth, and
every tongue confess that Jesus Christ is Lord, to the glory of
God the Father* (Philippians 2:5-11).

Because of Jesus' humility and His willingness to submit to the authority of the Father, the Father in turn exalted Him as the all-powerful, pre-eminent ruler of all things. The religious leaders could only pretend to have anything like that.

Coming Alive to His Authority

All the experts on culture tell us that young men and women in the Western world despise the idea of being under authority nowadays. According to them and their research, there is a general distrust of all forms of authority, from powerful centralized government authority to local municipal authority. Political scandals, corporate greed, upheaval in the Catholic Church over the sexual misconduct of priests, and the public failure of evangelical leaders like Jim Bakker, Jimmy Swaggart, and Ted Haggard have added to the distrust and dislike of authority figures. It's just not cool, trendy, or in style to voluntarily submit yourself to authority in today's cultural climate. Is there any authority we can fully trust in light of all the abuse we're so familiar with?

Actually, there is a kind of authority that's altogether different from what we have been exposed to. It is a loving authority that has our best interest at heart. It is the authority of Christ.

The more we see Jesus, the more we study Jesus, and the more we follow Jesus, the more we come alive to His ultimate authority over us in every area of our lives. As Christ becomes clearer to us, our love for Him and His kingdom grows, and the desire for the meaningless things of this world diminishes. You could say that earthly appetites "die" as our desire to walk in the ways of Jesus "comes alive." In a very real way, death in one arena of life brings forth life in another. We are dying to live. His authority over us as Lord is not offensive or to be avoided, but rather becomes desirable and is to be embraced with joy!

The first time I was ever pulled over by a police officer was unforgettable. I was a football player in the best shape of my life. I was strong and cocky. When the blue lights began flashing and I pulled over to the shoulder of the highway, a very small highway patrolman walked over to my door. He asked me to exit the vehicle and produce my driver's license and registration. When I stood beside him on the road, I was amazed at how much bigger I was than him. I was almost a foot taller, I outweighed him by at least 80 pounds. I could have easily taken him had we decided to throw fisticuffs.

But the moment he handed me a ticket, I realized the difference between the two of us. I had power. He had authority.

Jesus entered a world of religious piety and hypocrisy. The very leaders who killed Him had arrived at their state of hypocrisy by assuming authority over the children of Israel not to serve them and lead them, but to use them and get rich off of them. The only thing they had was power. The Romans and the Jewish religious leaders had this in common.

The physical power I had to beat up the patrolman did not equate to the moral or judicial authority to beat up the patrolman. He had the entire state government behind him when he issued me a ticket. Just because the Romans had the power to collect taxes from Jewish peasants didn't mean it was right or ethical. Just because they had the power to kill Jesus didn't mean they had authority over Him at all. Just because the Pharisees had power to keep peasants poor by extorting money from them did not give them authority to break God's law. The one who can kill may have momentary power, but the One who judges all hearts and motives and hands down eternal mercy and punishment has the authority.

Richard Horsley comments on the authority of Christ as He spoke prophetically on behalf of the marginalized and weak.

> In both his actions and teaching Jesus opposed the Roman imperial order and its effects on subject peoples. The Roman elite assumed that since they possessed the power, they could use it to subject other peoples of the world and to extract resources from them. Peoples who dared oppose the Roman imperial order were simply terrorized with intimidating military violence. Imperial consequences left villages devastated, families disrupted, and survivors traumatized.[4]

The most famous sermon Christ ever preached is now called the Sermon on the Mount. Jesus taught on a hillside above the Sea of Galilee. The audience was filled with poor Jewish peasants, fishermen, hardscrabble farmers, and plain everyday Jews. They lived far from Jerusalem and the temple. Yet they were still told what to do by the religious pros, who never ventured north to their neck of the woods or cared enough about them to tax them proportionately according to their income. So the words of Christ spoken to them early on in His earthly ministry were refreshing and strange because He spoke authoritatively. Perhaps they were simply impressed that a rabbi would actually sit down with them and be there, physically, instead of passing down orders from headquarters. His gentle authority impressed them, considering their distaste and even bitterness toward the corrupt system they were accustomed to. Hear what they said:

> *When Jesus had finished saying these things, the crowds were amazed at his teaching, because he taught as one who had authority, and not as their teachers of the law* (Matthew 7:28-29).

Jesus was able to speak and act with authority precisely because He was *under* authority! He submitted Himself to the will of His Father and in doing so, became more powerful, not less powerful. This message is anathema to us, not only to the average middle-class American wage earner, but even to the typical seminarian or youth pastor. "No, no, no!" we are told by the media and the specialists. We cannot tell young people to submit to authority, because our postmodern worldview rejects any such delineation between leaders and followers. Young professionals are told they don't work "for" a company; they work "at" a company. New business books tell executives not to refer to themselves as "bosses" or "superiors" but to instead call themselves "business associates" or "colleagues."

> We simply cannot follow Jesus unless we are willing to admit His authority and submit to His authority.

While I have no desire to resurrect traditional workplace terminology from days gone by, I simply want to point out that the idea of anyone, anywhere, ever having authority (the right to tell us what to do and the expectation that we should do it) over us is not only old-fashioned, it has become just plain offensive. This is too bad for us Christians. Even though it's against our sinful, selfish nature to be inclined toward submission to authority, we simply cannot follow Jesus unless we are willing to admit His authority and submit to His authority. When we convert to faith in Him, we are under new ownership.

Indeed, our very identity is wrapped up in a phrase that flies in the face of all modern and postmodern philosophies of being the masters of our destinies, of being independent individuals whose greatest pursuit in life is self-fulfillment and whose core value is simply valuing self above all else.

The one phrase that defines the Christian life is so countercultural that most churches don't even embrace it beyond a trite T-shirt or bumper sticker. It is a simple three-word phrase that changed history: *Jesus is Lord.*

CHAPTER 6

Jesus Is Lord

A DEAR OLD FRIEND of mine who has now passed away had great wealth. One of the things he loved to do was entertain. He was generous with his earnings and decided to build a great big house, one large enough to host feasts and gatherings of all sorts. Seldom did a weekend go by without a cohort of people descending on the "big house" for singing, fellowship, eating, laughing, and good times. One of my fondest memories is joining his family with my wife and our entire ministry at their home, first eating and then moving into their giant living room, where we sang our hearts out! We sang choruses and old hymns, and each of us felt God in that room. My friend's wealth was spent in the worship of Jesus Christ.

This man died several years ago, and everyone who knew him was heartbroken. Yet when we speak of him today, it is not sadness that overcomes us. On the contrary, it is joy! We remember his kindness, his bold laughter, his winsome personality, and how the air was filled with love and celebration and generosity when we all gathered at his house for a meal and singing. He lived in such a way that even after his body was dead, his legacy and testimony lived on. Though dead (in the flesh), he lives (in spirit). This is precisely because he conducted his life in a way that was dead to, oblivious to, and nearly immune to the trappings of his own accomplishments. And that's why he now lives on in our memories and conversations as a shining example of someone who died to live. His life continues long after his body was laid to rest.

Whose Glory?

Some people use their good fortune for the benefit of others and the glory of God. Others use their riches to prove their wealth in a display of their own glory.

The Caesars were the latter. The Roman emperors claimed to be directly picked by the gods to rule and reign in glory over the people of the earth. This idea grew and metastasized until the emperors eventually claimed to be gods. Not just picked and sent by the gods. They were gods in themselves. They claimed to be divine. Inscribed on coins and on great structures were the words "Caesar is Lord." Roman citizens were even expected to recite these three words if they ever came face-to-face with a Roman official or soldier on the street. "Caesar is Lord" became a Roman slogan that everyone was familiar with and that everyone would eventually say at some point in their life, whether they believed it or not.

The Caesars, however, believed it. And they lived like it was true.

When Julius Caesar, or any one of his successors for that matter, called for a party, they spared no expense. Their parties were carefully planned and perfectly executed endeavors of propaganda and megalomania. They wanted all of Rome and her richest, most powerful, most influential citizens to realize the glory and splendor that belonged to the Caesar.

If Caesar was Lord, then his parties were proof.

A date of a great banquet would be announced via courier, much as in the parable Jesus told in Luke 14. Only the most prominent public figures were extended an invitation to these great feasts, to be held at the residence of the Caesar himself. War heroes and victorious generals, wealthy landowners and tycoons, career politicians and entertainers, these were all personally invited by the emperor to attend. And the feasts were no small undertaking. They took a month to plan and prepare because these banquets lasted for days.

One of the luxuries of antiquity was meat. Food had to be killed or harvested, then cleaned, prepared, and cooked. Only the super-rich could afford it, so the emperor would have tables filled with beef and pork, lamb and fowl and fish—not so everyone would know how kind he was, but so everyone would know how rich he was. The banquets made the statement that he alone had the ability to entertain and feed the nation's elite. Only a god could do such things.

Other considerations were taken into account, such as entertainment. What would a party be without music and dancing? Musicians, jesters, dancers, and singers were located throughout the gardens, and while people ate the choicest food and got drunk on the finest wines, they reveled in laughter and dancing and music. The entertainment was 'round the clock. (Sounds much like a cruise ship.)

And as delicate as the subject may be, we dare not leave out the ladies whose services were acquired and paid for by the emperor. In a final show of goodwill toward his political supporters and faithful military men who had been asked to attend the party, the Caesar made sure there was plenty of love to go around. Beautiful women were on call to satisfy the sexual fantasies of the attendees, all paid for by the god of Rome, the emperor himself. He spared no expense. He was a host who really did think of everything.

He wanted everyone to go home talking about him, his gardens and mansion, his servants and slaves, the food and the wine and the music and the glory that was the Caesar. The message was simply this: All good things come from the emperor. He supplies everyone's needs. He cares for Rome and her people. And he caters to the rich and powerful. How could Rome survive without its lord, without Caesar?

So you see, if you were lucky enough to be invited to one of these great feasts, you would be a fool to turn down the invitation.

Unless you were a Christian.

The Moment When Everything Changed

As a sort of sick combination of entertainment and political state-ment, Christians and their families were brought to Caesar's feasts, not to indulge in the debauchery, but to become public spectacles of ridi-cule and derision. The thinking went this way: *Let's bring some Chris-tians to our big parties. They will most likely take one good look at all the food and wine and festivities and deny Jesus on the spot. Who would give up tangible, immediate benefits for unseen, unproven faith in a dead man? If they don't capitulate, we can just kill them.*

There was a kind of protocol that existed upon arrival at these feasts. A crier would announce your name, giving you a feeling of importance and pride as you prepared to enter the feast. But first you had to actu-ally stand in front of Caesar, who greeted all guests personally—an act of arrogance flowing from a desire to be seen and honored more than to welcome. Dressed in all his finest, the emperor would stand behind a small altar, flanked on his right and left by two of the biggest and baddest soldiers in all of Rome. These were his security detail and were meant to intimidate. With royal regalia and a golden garland on his head, Caesar stood behind the altar, which contained a small bronze basin filled with incense. In front of that basin was a small fire.

To be granted admission required a small act of worship. Individu-als had to take a pinch of the incense from the basin, throw it into the flames of the fire, which released a puff of smoke and a pleasing aroma, and look at Caesar. They were to bow their heads, lift their hands to their sides with palms open, and recite the Roman slogan that had now become common throughout the empire.

Caesar is Lord.

Another little reminder to all the powerful, rich, elite movers and shakers that came to the banquet. It is Caesar who made this hap-pen. He invited you. He has all authority. And before you engage in a weeklong drunken orgy of pleasure, remember—you are not Lord. Caesar is.

As a show of the emporer's strength and ruthlessness, Christians were marched up to the alter. The expectation was simple. Just look at Caesar, throw the incense into the fire, drop your head, lift your hands, and say the magic words.

Caesar is Lord.

Then you prove you really don't believe in Jesus at all. You are free to enter the feast, eat and drink all you want, but no more foolishness about Jesus. Thank you very much.

It is here, right here, where I believe all of history changed. This was the moment where, using a geological term, the tectonic plates shifted. It was right here, during the reigns of Vespasian and Diocletian and Nero and others, where the momentary empire of Rome began to crumble and the eternal kingdom of God broke through on earth via the church. It was a simple confession of faith in Jesus that turned the tide of world history:

> *If you confess with your mouth, "Jesus is Lord," and believe in your heart that God raised him from the dead, you will be saved* (Romans 10:9).

Never underestimate the power of your words to change people, change circumstances, change history. The apostle Paul probably had no idea how his words to the church in Rome, written in a letter that was read out loud in homes and at meals among Christians, would have ripple effects for thousands of years. It seems that his admonition in Romans 10:9 had sunk deep into the hearts of Christians, who were now faced with a life-or-death dilemma. When brought before the emperor, what should they do?

Should they recite the slogan in order to live? What if they just said it with their mouth but in their hearts were saying they loved Jesus? Would that be okay?

What would be better...to refuse to say the slogan and be killed on the spot, or to just say it, get it over with, and be free to return home to your family and your community, where you could tell more people the gospel of the resurrection of Jesus Christ? Certainly God would understand that it made more practical sense to sort of cross your fingers behind your back, say the slogan (it was just three words, for crying out loud!), and live another 30 or 40 years sharing the story of Jesus. What good would anyone be to God if they were dead? After all, dead people can't testify about Jesus.

> Did that mean he would be killed on the spot but Jesus would save him by raising him from the dead just seconds after he was killed?

Or maybe they can. Even 2000 years after they are dead.

At some point, a Christian stood before the emperor. That Christian heard the words of Paul in his mind. The promise of that verse is that salvation comes to those who confess that Jesus is Lord. Not Caesar. Not Rome. Not the empire. Jesus is Lord—which means no one else, nothing else can be. Caesar might be able to kill you, but he can't save you. Jesus can save you. Jesus can give you life if you are willing to lose it for Him. And that first Christian martyr standing before the emperor had to decide if he believed what Paul had said—that no matter what consequence awaited him for his refusal to bow to Rome, Jesus would save him. Would he die to live?

Would Jesus save him in that very moment, right after he refused the slogan? Did that mean he would be killed on the spot but Jesus would save him by raising him from the dead just seconds after he was killed? Did that mean that once he died for his refusal, his soul would be transported to heaven, where he would be with Jesus forever, eternally saved? He probably had no idea exactly what it meant. The one thing he did know was the truth.

The truth. Caesar was not Lord. Jesus was. He could not lie. He would bow to no one but the risen Christ. If he died as a result of this belief, he would live; he would live on in heaven and he would live on as testimony to those who remained—that Christ had died to live and so must those who follow Him.

Dying to live did not begin in your lifetime or mine. Christians have been dying to live for nearly 2000 years.

So this first martyr, whoever he (or she) was, stood before the man who claimed to be god. And instead of throwing the offering of incense into the fire and reciting the Roman slogan, he turned his back to Caesar.

Instead of bowing his head, he lifted his head toward heaven.

Instead of dropping his hands to his sides, lifting his palms, and saying "Caesar is Lord," he lifted his arms high, his hands reaching up.

Instead of remaining silent and saying nothing at all, he replaced the lie with the truth and vocalized it. He said three words that became the first confession of faith of the Christian church. Three words that were spiritual and political, personal and true. Three words that very literally changed the trajectory of human history. Three words Paul had admonished them to say.

JESUS IS LORD.

JESUS IS LORD!

Did he say it just once? Was she timid at first? Did he barely manage to whisper it? Did one of the Roman bodyguards, in disbelief have to ask him to repeat himself? Did she say it four or five times? Did he get louder with each repetition? Was he screaming it at the top of his lungs at the very end?

Without hesitation or deliberation, the Roman guard drew his sword from its scabbard and with one smooth motion removed the head of the Christian from its body.

Death was immediate. Life, however, was just as immediate—and also eternal.

The martyr had died to live. He found life by losing it. The moment his eyes closed in this world, they opened wide in the next world. And they saw Jesus, the real Lord of all.

This was the moment when everything changed. A precedent had been set. At the altar to the divinity of Caesar, blood was spilled because of one person's faith in Jesus. This small event, in essence, began a butterfly effect because of which the Roman Empire would one day crumble. It also became a catalyst for the worldwide spread of the gospel and expansion of the church. Everything changed.

Nobody knows how many Christians lost their lives this way, or how many were slaughtered in the Coliseum as entertainment, or how many were burned alive, cut into pieces, fed to wild animals, or sold as slaves. But 200 years later, the Roman Empire was filled with followers of Christ, growing exponentially faster than could even be counted. As the foundations of a debauched and tyrannical culture were groaning under its weight, an unstoppable force was gaining momentum. It was the church. And it was filled with people whose allegiance was to the Lord Jesus Christ, the only true God and the only Lord.

They had proven they were not afraid to die. It was indeed their deaths that had brought life to the world, salvation to the sinner, and hope to humanity. Dying to live became the paradox by which Christians testified to the power of the gospel. The more they were beaten, bruised, and killed, the faster they grew and multiplied. Though it seemed counterintuitive, death brought life and growth and conversion. As believers in Jesus were tortured throughout the empire and murdered in cold blood or for sport and entertainment, they scattered from place to place, town to town, telling the story of Jesus everywhere they stopped.

So the Roman plan backfired. By killing Christians, they did not kill Christianity. They assisted in its growth. The more Christians died, the more they lived. The church exploded in the face of persecution, and even because of it! Christians were dying and the church was living! The same paradox that applies to the individual lives of Christians also applies to the body of Christ, the church. Dying to live works on both fronts.

Within a few short years, the Roman Empire would be split into two halves, and a few more centuries would see its total demise. As the empire waned, becoming old and decrepit, the church waxed strong and deep as it spread to the ends of the earth. All because a small, marginalized, poor band of believers stood firm by their deepest of convictions to the death. All because some ordinary people heard an extraordinary story and believed it. All because some common folks found life by dying, first to their sin, and then, literally and physically, embracing death for the promise of eternal life.

✝

Jesus was Lord then. Jesus is Lord now. And He is worth dying and living for. And if we live for Him, then no matter how we leave this life, we will have died for Him. And our death will bring life to those who come after us, long after our memories have vanished from the earth and kingdoms have risen and fallen. The testimony of those who believe that Jesus is Lord outlives and outshines any empire or kingdom of man.

Jesus is Lord. Find true life by losing everything to gain Him. Die to yourself so you can live in and through Christ!

CHAPTER 7

Beaten, Bruised, and Blessed: Sharing in Christ's Sufferings

EARLY ON IN MY YOUNG LIFE as a Christian, I was privileged to have a real-life experience that changed everything for me. I'd read the words of Jesus concerning finding life by losing it. I had even, believe it or not, preached on it myself, even though I had no idea what it really meant to die to myself. The concept was there in theory. I needed to see it in reality. God allowed me to do just that at the tender age of 18. I saw the paradox of "dying to live" take on flesh and blood right in front of me.

I began preaching in 1987 and began traveling outside the United States in 1991. My first mission trip was to Jamaica and, truth be told, I signed up for two reasons: I honestly wanted to go build a church in the mountains of Jamaica, and I honestly thought it would be cool to visit an island country and spend some time kicking back on the beach. I was in for many, many surprises.

I had never seen poverty before, not like that. I had never felt heat before, not like that. I had never known fatigue before, not like that. After the first day in the Windsor district of the Jamaican mountains, it dawned on me that the call of God on my life to follow Him in ministry was not going to always be easy. This was my first taste of dying to my selfish ways. We had no air conditioning. We had no soft drinks. We didn't get ice in our water. And I mixed cement all day long in the Jamaican sun with a shovel and then preached for a solid two hours for the Jamaican church in the evenings. I survived, but I was 18 years old at the time. I'm not sure my body could do it anymore. But as a teenager, I made it, though barely.

During those long, hot days, I became fast friends with two Jamaican boys about my age who both lived in the community where we were building the church. Their names were Garfield and Mark. We mixed cement all day long for a week and our shared suffering and sweat created a bond of sorts. We ate together and shared stories about our families. They asked dozens of questions about America. We told jokes and laughed at each other. I told them of my conversion to faith in Christ and how God was transforming me into a new person. A special friendship was formed during those days around the cement pit.

God was gracious and both of these young men repented of their sins that week at the church where I was preaching each night. Garfield came to the altar in tears, weeping and crying out to God for mercy. Mark responded two nights later but without the slightest sign of emotion or grief. He never shed a tear. He just said he wanted to follow Jesus and become a Christian, so we prayed with him and gave him a Bible and said we would see him the next morning at the job site, where we would mix another 67 tons of cement.

Mark did not show up for work the next morning. We didn't worry at first, but by lunchtime no one had heard from him, so Garfield went to his house to see if he was there. He returned with bad news. Mark had had a big fight last night after church with his father. His father was angry and drunk but no one knew where Mark was. We stopped and prayed for Mark right there around the cement pit and then went back to work.

Several hours later I stood up to preach, dehydrated and exhausted from a week of the hardest physical labor I had ever known to that point in my life. My head ached and my joints hurt and my skin was on fire from the sunburn, and my palms were covered in blisters, and so were my feet. But somehow God's grace empowered me and I was able to deliver a message, though I can't remember what it was about or even what passage I preached from. Then about halfway through the message, I saw Mark slip in and sit on the very back row. It was very dark—there were only a few torches, and there were no walls in that tabernacle. It had a few posts and a tin roof and was overflowing with people. But once I saw Mark, I couldn't quit looking at him. I knew something was terribly wrong.

Just as soon as we dismissed the service, I went directly to him. He waited for me. When I approached, Garfield was already there. We asked him where he had been all day and told him we had been worried. His response shook me to my core because I had never met anyone who had actually suffered for Christ. I had only read about them in books. I was about to see firsthand for the first time what it meant to

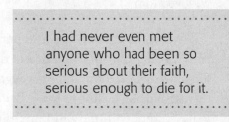

I had never even met anyone who had been so serious about their faith, serious enough to die for it.

find life by losing it. I still remember what he said to us when we asked what had happened.

"When I went home last night, I was so happy because I had given my heart to Jesus like you and Garfield. I told my family that I was a Christian and that I wanted to be a preacher and tell every village in Jamaica about Jesus and salvation. But my father became very angry. He told me I could not be a Christian and live in his home. This was evil, he said, and he forbid me to come back to this place to work or to hear preaching. I told him that I could not stay away, that you are my family now, and he said that he would beat it out of me. I told him it was not possible to beat Jesus out of my heart, and he said he would show me.

"So he took a long stick and he hit me many times, so hard, all over my body. From my head to my feet. For maybe five minutes. I knew he was going to kill me but I did not care because I was saved, I knew I would go to heaven and be with Jesus. Then when I could not stand up anymore, he told me to leave his home and never come back. I was dead to him and no longer his son. So I left and slept under the pine-apple trees all night and today until I could get the strength to come back to church tonight."

I could not believe what I was hearing. I had been a believer for four years but had never known persecution or sacrifice like that. I had never even met anyone who had been so serious about their faith, se-rious enough to die for it. But there was no sorrow or remorse in his voice or in his eyes. His face was illuminated with joy, and the very peace of Christ flowed from his tongue when he spoke. Garfield and I put our arms around him and prayed for him and told him how much we loved him.

I still think about Mark and pray for him. It has been many years since I've heard from either one of those young men, but I won't soon forget what God showed me through Mark and his testimony. I saw an 18-year-old boy willing to lose his life just because he had found life in Jesus. It stuck with me and I am still wrestling with it to this very day. Maybe he tapped into this great paradox...

> *Then he called the crowd to him along with his disciples and said: "If anyone would come after me, he must deny himself and take up his cross and follow me. For whoever wants to save his life will lose it, but whoever loses his life for me and for the gospel will save it"* (Mark 8:34-35).

Surrounded by witch doctors and voodoo, Mark had to pay a se-vere price and live with some serious consequences for even claiming to follow Jesus. There was no middle ground in the world he lived in. Claiming to believe in Christ as Lord did not endear him to a com-munity or open up business opportunities for him like it does in other parts of the world. His faith came with a heavy price tag. The thought never occurred to him to just deny Christ to save his own skin. Though that would have had a greater benefit in the moment, he had been transformed at a deep level. The change was irreversible and undeniable. Christ had spared him from spiritual death and given him life.

He was then ready to face physical death if that was what was required of him by Jesus. He did not whine. He did not complain. He did not ask why. He just faced the pain and humiliation and isolation as a natural result of forsaking all things in order to gain Jesus. Just a day after meeting Jesus, Mark understood more about the paradox of dying to live than most Christians learn in a lifetime. I think of him now when I read these words from Paul, written to his friends in the church in Philippi:

> *I want to know Christ and the power of his resurrection and the fellowship of sharing in his sufferings, becoming like him in his death, and so, somehow, to attain to the resurrection from the dead* (Philippians 3:10-11).

CHAPTER 8

Come and Die

I SERVE MANY ROLES in the kingdom of God. I am an author, a missionary, an evangelist, and a pastor.

I serve as teaching pastor at NewSpring Church in South Carolina. The pastor is one of my closest, lifelong friends. His name is Perry, and as the church has grown to 15,000 people and multiple campuses, Perry and the leadership of the church have adopted a new bold mission statement for NewSpring.

Come and See. Come and Die.

Catchy? Yep. Easy to remember? Sure. But more than anything, it encapsulates the call of a disciple. Both the disciples that followed Jesus 2000 years ago and the billions of disciples who claim Him as Lord today.

Come and see. See this man who is unlike any other. See this man who can walk on water and raise the dead. See this man who speaks with authority to the corruption of the religious professionals. See this man who knows things He shouldn't know. See this man who looks like an ordinary Hebrew carpenter but lives and speaks and acts like a prophet. See this man who is none other than the living God.

This is the first call of Jesus.

Come and see Me. I am loving, full of grace and mercy. My compassion for you never ends. My patience is limitless. See My miracles. See My power. Experience the emotional freedom of being accepted by Me just like you are. See what God looks like by looking at Me. See how I can change lives from the inside out by looking at how I have transformed the lives of those who follow Me. Come and see what you have never seen before, and you will be changed by what you see.

The second call of Jesus is vastly different. The action required is much harsher than seeing. It is dying.

Come and die.

Come and die to your meaningless pursuit of what you want.

Die to killing yourself in order to gain those possessions you think you cannot live without.

Die to the daily rat race of collecting more money, collecting more debt, and collecting more anxiety about how to manage what you collect.

Die to your constant feelings of insecurity, inadequacy, and competitiveness.

Die to the envy you feel when others have more than you have.

Die to the bitterness you hold toward those who have hurt or abandoned you.

Die to the death that pulses through your veins as you work harder and harder in your fruitless race to find significance apart from Me and the cross I died upon.

Once you die to trying to do it all alone, then you will have found life, because then you will have become My disciple.

It's easy to draw a crowd when all you offer them is something cool to watch. Like an exciting movie. Anyone can do that. But when you start talking about denying yourself, dying to your selfish impulses, putting to death your sinful desires, giving someone else total authority to call the shots in your life, then the numbers do a nosedive and the crowds begin to disperse. It is what happened with Jesus. He had massive rallies everywhere that He healed and fed people. But when He began talking about the radical call of discipleship and the high price of following Him as Lord (see John 6), the hordes dwindled to a few. As His death approached, only a handful remained. Finally, at Golgotha, only John was with Him, caring for Mary, the mother of Jesus. Even Peter, the big fisherman with a big mouth and an even bigger foot to put in it, had denied Jesus and run away.

Yet it was with this small number of men, 11 of the original 12, that Jesus established His church and began a movement that is more unstoppable today than it has ever been.

Do you really think that if you want to follow Him, He will lower His expectations for you? He will ask the exact same thing from you that He has asked from everyone who has ever been His disciple.

Come and die.

Grace: Cheap or Costly?

That which is gained too easily is valued too lightly.

I'm not sure who came up with that little nugget (probably Winston Churchill or Teddy Roosevelt), but it rings true. I learned this lesson well at age 15. If I had only believed it when my father told me. Of course, I had to learn the hard way.

My daddy bought me a 1986 Ford Bronco II. He said it was the only car he would ever buy for me, and that if I wrecked and destroyed it, then I could either buy another vehicle on my own or ride with my mom everywhere. Or walk.

Then he predicted the outcome. "I am going to regret getting you this car, I just know it. Most boys your age tear up a few cars before they learn to respect one."

Just like Nostradamus, he peered into the crystal ball and saw my future, because exactly four months after I received the Bronco, I flipped it on a dirt road. A total loss. The words he spoke to me that afternoon, after coming to get me and driving me home in silence from the crash site, struck a deep note of truth.

"Well, son, I am thankful you are alive. But I meant what I said. You will be responsible for all your vehicles from now on. And you know what? I bet you will take care of the next one because you will have to pay for it with your own money. You will treat it better than one somebody gives to you, because the gift doesn't cost you anything."

He was absolutely, categorically, correct.

That which is gained too easily is valued too lightly.

The Bronco was history and I had to get another means of transportation. The 1979 Camaro I purchased for $2400 cash lasted me until I went to college, and I could not have loved a car more than that one. It was old and worn out and averaged seven miles to the gallon. But I esteemed that car. I had bought it. That was hard-earned cash sitting in my driveway. I had paved driveways for that money. I had tarred the roof of my dad's motor shop for that money. I had split firewood and packed copper wire in 55-gallon drums all summer in a 100-degree warehouse for that money. I valued that Camaro more than the Bronco, even though the Bronco had more value than the Camaro.

> I saw a free gift that could be used and abused. It was valuable, but to me it was cheap. I had paid nothing for it.

When I looked at the Camaro, I saw hard work and sweat and sore muscles. All the jobs I'd done and all the work and labor expended brought me a respect and reverence for the vehicle that became my new transportation. I valued a car with relatively little real value.

When I looked at the Bronco, I saw a free gift that could be used and abused. It was valuable, but to me it was cheap. I had paid nothing for it.

There is a strong, strong connection between the Christian who has suffered greatly for Jesus and the God he or she has suffered for. The greater the sacrifice, the greater the affection. The more one loses in order to follow Jesus, the more one seems to love Jesus. The more one loses, the more one gains. In losing more of myself, I find more of Christ. Christ in me, the hope of glory.

Costly Grace Says "Come and Die"

In his monumental *Cost of Discipleship,* the German pastor and theologian Dietrich Bonhoeffer confronts the Christian church with the concept of costly grace versus cheap grace. Along with C.S. Lewis and Billy Graham, few have influenced my theology or worldview as much as Bonhoeffer.

For Bonhoeffer, cheap grace was trying to take all the blessings that God promises you in Christ with no consequences. In his words, cheap grace is Christianity without discipleship. In describing this skewed view of the grace of God, he says,

> Instead of following Christ, let the Christian enjoy the consolations of his grace. That is what we mean by cheap grace, the grace that amounts to the justification of sin without the justification of the repentant sinner, who departs from sin and from whom sin departs. Cheap grace is not the kind of forgiveness of sin that frees us from the toils of sin. Cheap grace is the grace we bestow on ourselves.[5]

Costly grace, on the other hand, was the call of Jesus upon all His true disciples to follow Him wherever He might lead, regardless of the consequences. In a self-fulfilling prophecy, Bonhoeffer said, "When Christ calls a man, He bids him come and die."

He had no way of knowing he would live out those words soon enough.

In describing costly grace, he says,

> Such grace is costly because it calls us to follow…It is costly because it costs a man his life…It is costly because it condemns sin…Above all, it is costly because it cost God the life of his Son…and what has cost God much cannot be

cheap for us. Above all, it is grace because God did not reckon his Son too dear a price to pay for our life, but delivered him up for us.[6]

Bonhoeffer was a German Lutheran pastor. A brilliant mind seemed to be his greatest tool at an early age—he received his PhD in his mid-20s. But it is not for his mind or intellect we remember him today. It is how he died and the way he lived until his death. He died in order to live.

This pastor with thin blonde hair and glasses was a pacifist. He subscribed to the resolution that in no circumstance would he as a Christian resort to any sort of physical violence. He could not serve in a war effort that required him to fire a weapon at the enemy. He would never willfully or knowingly strike or harm a person. This was his conviction as a young man, and it is important in regard to how his life ended.

Bonhoeffer's masterpiece *The Cost of Discipleship* is almost painful to sit and read because every word drips with the stinging conviction that I myself have not completely embraced what it means to live the crucified life Jesus modeled for me. Bonhoeffer exposes "cheap grace" as a sham; a faith that does not require someone to die to their sin and their selfishness is no faith at all. A faith that does not require discipleship is a faith not worth having. He bases this conviction on the life and ministry of Jesus. Bonhoeffer's theology can best be summed up in the famous quote that I have used countless times in sermons and not nearly enough times on myself.

"When Christ calls a man, He bids him come and die."

There is no salvation without death. There is no discipleship without death. But this death is not an end. It is a beginning—the beginning of life! And it is not just the death of Jesus on the cross we are speaking of. It is our death to the old nature, to sin and smugness, to pride and self-righteousness and stubborn self-sufficiency, which allows us to follow our leader who gave us life by His death. And that is how we find life. Through His death. And the resulting death we experience is to all that is evil and diabolical in us. We find life in embracing death. Jesus' death and our death. From His death springs our life.

A Costly Death

Bonhoeffer's pacifist convictions came early in his life. They were challenged when a man burst on the scene in his native Germany, a man who captivated the attention and angst of a nation that had been shamed and embarrassed on the international stage after World War I. Germany had been stripped of its national pride and was treated with utter disrespect by the world community and the victors in the war. A collective bitterness grew among the German population, and the stage had been set for a string of events that would change history.

A charismatic and confident art-school dropout named Adolf Hitler began spewing nationalistic rhetoric to the people, and his populist ideas fanned the aspirations of a once-great nation that wanted to lead the world again as a bastion of intellect, military might, the arts, and philosophy. With enthralling speeches and a near-demonic sway over the masses, Hitler was ultimately given complete control over the nation of Germany. He put people to work, built a massive military, and became dictator. He was all-powerful. And even the German churches almost unanimously embraced his promise of restoring the glory and honor to their nation. It is haunting to see old photographs from the late 1930s where Hitler is flanked by pastors and bishops and church officials, everyone all smiles, hands gripped together in a show of support and solidarity for a man who would prove to be a liar, a killer, and a demoniac.

Bonhoeffer had come to America in 1930 for a year's study. While there, in Harlem to be exact, he had worshipped with African-American believers and heard in their sermons and songs about the blessing of suffering as a people for freedom and liberty. In 1939 he returned to New York, in part to escape some of the pressures that were being leveled against dissenters in Germany. The Nazi government was bullying the church. There was no more free press, and anyone who spoke against the Führer risked arrest. In America, enjoying freedom but thinking about his own people, Dietrich knew he had to go back to Germany. The thought of remaining safe across the Atlantic Ocean while his countrymen suffered was more than he could bear.

Upon his return, he had to contend with a serious question: If Jesus were alive today, would He remain a pacifist in the face of such great suffering and death, or would He act to stop it? Bonhoeffer concluded that it was more evil to do nothing than to use force in an attempt to stop a madman with the appetite to murder millions. He heard the call deep in his heart.

"When Christ calls a man, He bids him come and die."

It was this choice that cost him his life. Bonhoeffer agreed to participate in a secret plot to kill Hitler. And how he wrestled and struggled with that choice! He even had to die to his own belief that force and violence could never be used. He realized that in exceptional situations, the only way to save lives from a violent killer is to oppose the killer aggressively, even violently.

The plot was, of course, unsuccessful. (The recent Hollywood blockbuster *Valkyrie*, starring Tom Cruise, is loosely based on the true story.) Hitler was not to die from a bomb planted in a briefcase under a desk. He was to die at his own hand in a hopeless suicide as the Russians and Allies encroached closer and closer upon his underground bunker in Berlin. But before that time, those involved in the plot were discovered, and they were dealt with harshly.

> Christ was worth it all. Death on the gallows meant the beginning of an eternal and unending life with the Jesus who had already died in his place.

Naked and not sorry, Bonhoeffer was marched to the gallows just months before the war ended, before Hitler would put a bullet in his own temple by pulling the trigger on a German-engineered pistol that would end the most infamous and wicked reign of the past thousand years. As Bonhoeffer faced certain death, all that he had written about, all that he had preached, and all that he had lived for, became an ultimate and undeniable reality. Christ was worth it all. Death on the gallows meant the beginning of an eternal and unending life with the Jesus who had already died in his place.

On April 9, 1945, at the young age of 39, he died at Flossenbürg prison, hanged on a gallows built for traitors. Since his homecoming, life has sprung from his death. Millions have read his story, been arrested by his conviction, and been forced to wrestle with the reality of the high cost of becoming a disciple of Jesus Christ. Spiritual life for many has come from the death of one, and that tree of life is still bearing fruit to this very moment, as you read about a martyr and hero you have never met who gave all he had. His life.

Dietrich Bonhoeffer had obeyed the call of Christ.

Come and follow. Come and die. And find Life.

We find life by losing it. By giving it to Jesus.

For whoever wants to save his life will lose it, but whoever loses his life for me will find it (Luke 9:23).

CHAPTER 9

Sin Manager vs. Selfless Martyr

I COULD GET REALLY, REALLY RICH if I wanted to. So could you. Others are doing it. In droves. All we need to do is tap into basic human nature and allow the law of supply and demand to work its monetary magic.

Basic human nature is, without argument, sinful. There are no perfect people. We all mess up, miss the mark, make mistakes, and sin. So if you are ever up late at night like I frequently am, you've noticed there are entire programs, even entire channels, dedicated to helping people manage their sin and the results of their sin. It is mind-boggling.

For people who cannot quit smoking, you can chew gum, smoke a smokeless cigarette, or put a nicotine patch on your arm. (You really do need to watch more TV if you have never seen these infomercials.)

For people who struggle with their weight and cannot seem to stop eating, there are pills you can swallow, creams you can rub on your skin, herbal teas from Asia you can brew and drink, and even battery-operated electronic stimulation ("shock") units that will zap that extra body fat without requiring you to ever break a sweat.

For those folks who spend money incessantly, have racked up thousands of dollars in debt on their credit cards, and risk losing their homes and cars because they shopped and spent money without any forethought of the consequences, there are law firms, nonprofit agencies, and consultants who will help you reduce that debt overnight (for a small fee).

And for that elite group of Americans who forgot to pay their taxes, thought they could outwit the IRS, or were just too busy to get around to filing by April 15, there are tax attorneys who will bail you out by settling your tax bill for mere pennies on the dollar.

So if you want to get rich quick, it's essential that you tap into a line of work that capitalizes on the sins of others. That is where the money is nowadays. Nobody talks about self-control. You'll never see an infomercial targeted at those who want to learn how to say "no" to bad habits like smoking, gluttony, lying, cheating on their taxes, or taking advantage of others. Sin sells, especially if you can get in on the products that people want as a result of their sin.

The Way of Power?

The gospel tells us, however, that Jesus doesn't operate like that when it comes to our sin. He doesn't want to manage your sin or capitalize on it. And neither should we.

Jesus made it very clear that He had come to set things on their head when He declared, "The Son of Man did not come to be served, but to serve and to give His life as a ransom for many." He assumed the position of selfless martyr. The Pharisees assumed the position of sin manager.

> The sin-management approach... is severely flawed and powerless to kill the old life and inaugurate a new life of transformation.

Author and preacher Dallas Willard has become rather famous for saying that God is not interested in behavior modification. Much of what passes for Christian discipleship is dressed-up legalism, an attempt to modify or alter personal behavior from the outside. In other words, the harder a person tries to change their actions on the outside with resolutions, commitments, fad diets, and promises, the more frustrated they get when they discover they have no power to actually change themselves.

The Pharisees tapped into this reality. They imposed long lists of rules that governed all religious and social activities of the common people. The people tried and tried to keep these rules but kept on breaking them. The Pharisees capitalized on this hopeless cycle, banking on the failure of the people to keep the rules. They heaped condemnation on the common people for their failures but provided some clever ways out of the impending doom.

They would demand sacrifices from the people—for God, of course—but they would deem the animal sacrifices brought by the common people unclean, unworthy, and unacceptable. Then they would conveniently offer their own special animals. They placed them outside the temple and priced them to make a profit. They made a killing. Simply being sin managers made them rich and powerful.

Richard Foster sums up the root issue with the sin-management approach employed by the Pharisees, pointing out why it is severely flawed and powerless to kill the old life and inaugurate a new life of transformation.

> Jesus teaches that we must go beyond the righteousness of
> the scribes and Pharisees (Matthew 5:20). Yet we need to
> see that their righteousness was no small thing. They were
> committed to following God in a way that many of us are
> not prepared to do. One factor, however, was always central to their righteousness: externalism. Their righteousness
> consisted in control over externals, often including the manipulation of others. The extent to which we have gone beyond the righteousness of the scribes and Pharisees is seen
> in how much our lives demonstrate the internal work of
> God upon the heart.[7]

Taking Advantage of Sin

The world will always have sin managers because the world is fallen and all its inhabitants are rotten, wicked sinners. Including me (and you). Since there is an endless supply of sin, as soon as someone finds a way to make money off of it or leverage the guilt associated with it for their own gain, the cycle begins. The Pharisees sold animals for sacrifice. The Catholic Church sold indulgences. Self-help books fly off the shelves as fast as they can be written, and the masses tune into religious programming that makes them feel better about their "issues" by telling them to blame their parents, their teachers, or their potty-training for everything bad in their life. Just as with the scribes of old, the focus today is on externalism. The sin manager tells you to find life by trying harder or paying more money or following more rules.

These only bring death, not life and freedom.

Perhaps you have found yourself thinking it would be easy to take a shortcut when it comes to sinful areas of your life. You would not be alone. I know I've thought about it. Plenty of times. Jesus did not believe in shortcuts. He believed in dealing with the source of the problem, not the symptoms of the problem. He went to the root of our sin and dealt with it definitively on the cross.

Oh, and by the way, sin managers expect to be served by the sinners. They make their living off the sinners. They rely on the rules and regulations they impose on the sinners to keep them coming back for more rules and regulations in hopes they will really change someday.

I met a lady in the mid-1990s who could not function without her sin manager. She was part of an extremely legalistic church where the pastor had established himself as the ultimate and supreme authority on every issue, even telling members of the congregation what they could wear. After I had spoken a message at a huge student event, she approached to inform me that none of the teenagers who had responded to the message during the invitation had been genuinely saved, because I had preached the sermon in blue jeans. Yep, blue jeans.

After I had argued with her briefly that God was not concerned with outer appearance but the heart, she seemed to be listening. But suddenly she said she would have to run my wardrobe by her pastor and, depending on his judgment call, we would know whether the students had really been saved that night.

Evidently, her pastor maintained control over his church members by creating a list of sins and then managing the people with that list.

The Pharisees had set themselves up in a similar manner. They assumed the position of sin manager. Instead of dealing with the source of sin (the wicked human heart), they took advantage of the sin of the people and kept them crippled with backbreaking rules, laws, regulations, and legalism. Does this sound like the right way to live and enjoy life? It sounds disgusting and depressing to me.

A Declaration of Freedom

In contrast, God did things totally backward.

Jesus was not a sin manager. Instead, He was a selfless martyr. Like all martyrs, He died for a cause. Unlike all martyrs, He died not only for a cause, but also because of people—for those people, on their behalf. He died not just to make a point but to make a transaction. He did not die as an example to be remembered. He died as the Savior to be worshipped.

And how strange that God would die! He could have chosen an entirely different method of transaction. He could have, I guess, snapped His fingers and changed things. He could have, I guess, clapped His hands and started over by vaporizing the old world with all of its depraved inhabitants and making a new one with perfect little shiny, happy people on it.

Jesus Himself said, "The Son of man came not to be served, but to serve, and to give his life as a ransom for many" (Matthew 20:28). Talk about a paradox. This may have sounded nice to Galilean Zealots because they took it as a kind of populist rhetoric. As rhetoric, though, it eventually ran out of steam, because even the disenfranchised who want to topple a corrupt government that cares little for its people will ultimately realize they need more than a compassionate teacher with nice ideas. To topple a government, you need someone with the power, the sheer authority, and the will for battle to uproot the status quo and usher in a new day, a new era, a new administration of power.

Ironically, this is precisely what Jesus did. But He did it precisely backward. He chose a way that nobody of any cultural or religious persuasion would have bet on. Kings and conquerors have big egos that need to be fed by big victories and big parades celebrating their conquests. Sin managers need hordes of people to depend on them for the short-term emotional catharsis that comes from momentary penance and the assurance of pardon. Jesus had His own way because He had a very different and distinct identity. He showed the world what could be gained through self-sacrifice, and He invited those who would so choose to join Him in His revolution. Die to your selfish ways and find life. Gain life by giving it away. This sounded like utter nonsense to some, but to those who would believe, it was the greatest declaration of freedom to ever be spoken.

The Paradox of True Power

Still today, Jesus shows a world obsessed with power that the kind of power they have seen in action, and indeed want for themselves, is not power at all, because it never really lasts. When power pushes others down, ignores human dignity, and asserts itself as the strongest dog on the block, that power eventually gorges itself to oblivion. It burns hot for a while but burns out, and another, similarly self-seeking power takes its place.

Jesus' power was a humble and quiet authority that came with a laser-sharp focus. Instead of wielding supreme control and demanding that the world and all its inhabitants adhere to His every whim (like the Caesars did), Jesus came as a servant with the intention of serving humanity. How? By meeting their greatest need.

Forgiving humanity of its sin and reconciling people to God.

How was this accomplished? Simple. In death. Death on a bloody Roman cross. Slaughtered between two death-row inmates. Hung naked in public while the crowd spit on Him and cursed His birth.

This is not what GOD is supposed to look like. God is supposed to be holy, shiny, strong, and regal. God is supposed to be in control, needing nothing, aware of all things at the same time. God is supposed to be giving orders, not taking them. God is supposed to be served, not doing the serving. And of all things, God should not be publicly humiliated and murdered. This is not what God is supposed to look like.

> At the core of all things Christian, before there were Catholics and Protestants and Pentecostals...there was Christ and there was the cross.

Or maybe this is EXACTLY what God is supposed to look like.

The great paradox of the Christian experience is seen at its very beginning. At the core of all things Christian, before there were Catholics and Protestants and Pentecostals, before study Bibles and marriage retreats and vacation Bible school, there was Christ and there was the cross. The selfless martyr is hammered onto beams of wood, the same beams ruthless crooks and killers had been hammered onto. Their blood, their hair, and their flesh still clung to the cracks of the splintered cross. Do you think Roman executioners took the time to sanitize these torture devices before sticking another criminal on them? This is how God died. This is how we live.

At the creation of Christianity we have Christ and His cross.

> Had Jesus died only as your example, he would be of no help to you at all. You would see from his life how to live, but you'd get nothing from him to make that possible. However, because Jesus died in your place for your sins, and because he rose to conquer death and bring life, both

as your divine Savior and human example, you now have
a new identity, new provision, and new process. Your new
identity is now in Christ, which has given you new potential for a new life in every area of your existence.[8]

If you miss that, you miss it all. And for us, Christ still speaks to us
from that cross, saying, "Come, follow Me." Follow His example. Be
willing to live in response to the cross. Enjoy the authentic transformation that happens deep inside of you, the transformation instigated
by the grace of God in Jesus. Rejoice that Christ doesn't try to manage
your sin but instead gets rid of it.

Jesus doesn't want to make bad people good. He wants to raise dead
people to life.

He will not manage your sin. He will kill it by defeating it. He will
crush it by absorbing all its ammunition on a filthy, disgusting cross.
That is the Jesus we follow. And if we follow Him, then we must go
where He went and do what He did.

"Let us also go, that we may die with Him."

It is possible you could spend your whole life participating in Christian events and activities but never hear a word from a stage or a pulpit
or a preacher urging you to follow the example of our sinless martyr, Jesus Christ, by making yourself last, lowest, and least among the
crowd. That doesn't change the reality that embracing His sacrifice in
repentance and faith is still the only way to life and salvation.

CHAPTER 10

Panic and Peace

WHEN WE CROSS THE LINE OF FAITH and begin to follow Jesus, we recognize that we have given total control of our destiny to someone we have never physically met or seen or spoken to. If we are honestly saved and converted, a sense of panic and fear will eventually grip our soul. Once we realize what we have done, that we have handed ourselves over to whatever sovereign plan God has for our future, be it ministry or parenthood, martyrdom or imprisonment, riches or poverty, the realization that we are not the boss anymore takes our breath away. We sense the paradox groaning as it becomes a reality. We are actually dying to live, gaining life by losing it to Christ. Bonhoeffer describes it well:

> Every man is called separately and must follow alone. But men are frightened of solitude, and they try to protect themselves from it by merging themselves in the society of their fellow men and in their material environment. It is Christ's will that he should be thus isolated, and that he should fix his eyes solely upon him.[9]

If you are to fully dedicate yourself to living in this paradox of dying daily to sin to gain the life of Christ, you will be broken and humbled again and again as the sinful nature collides with your new heart. Once this fear sets in, panic is quick to follow. But right on the heels of that panic is a perfect peace—a peace that says you can trust the One who gave it all for you. He is in control now and you are better off with Him in charge than yourself. Panic and peace, together, seemingly conflicting with one another yet co-existing in the context of faith. I compare it to something that happened to me at a very young age, when I experienced these two conflicting emotions simultaneously.

✢

Just about everything good that I know or that I am, I learned from my father. I call him Daddy. He is an altogether different kind of human being, and is from an altogether different place historically and culturally than you can probably understand. Born at the beginning of World War II, he lived in crippling poverty that would render a modern-day family powerless. But people back then, in general, were much tougher and more resourceful, not to mention simpler in their daily needs. As a boy, Daddy lived in a home without electricity or running water. The family grew or slaughtered all their food, except for the occasional bag of sugar or salt they needed at the general store, and then they seldom paid for those with cash. They instead traded for such staple items with eggs or milk or butter from the farm.

I have always wished I could have lived in that day, and could have known my daddy then, and been his friend. I think we would have been the closest of companions. We would have rambled in the woods together, hunted and fished together, and gotten into every sort of mischief available to us. As I grow older and have a family of my own, I find myself needing him more now than ever before—his advice, support, understanding, and presence.

Our close relationship was built on a foundation Daddy laid early on. We did things together: We worked in the fields, we planted and plowed corn, we cut firewood and cut grass. We played together: He came to my practices and ball games, took me hunting, told me stories, and threw the football with me after work in the front yard. It was during one of our outdoor adventures that I experienced the very emotions the Christian feels when they awaken to the paradox of finding life by losing, by giving it away to Jesus. I was overcome with a sort of panic I had never known as my daddy and I walked together in the big woods.

Deer season was right around the corner, and we hunted on a gigantic piece of land about an hour from our home. We drove there one afternoon to scout some hot spots and hopefully find a good place to hunt in the fall. With tens of thousands of acres to explore, we could spend days in there. We saw tracks and deer sign, so much of it, in fact, that we lost track of where we were going. We just kept walking, amazed at how many deer were in the area, until Daddy realized we were lost. For a few minutes I believe he tried to keep it from me, but I could tell something wasn't right. I also realized that in all the years we had been in the woods together, I had never seen this area, and I doubted that he had ever been there either.

Finally, after an hour of walking in no apparent direction, he fessed up. And for the first time in my young life, I saw fear in my father's face.

"Well, son, I don't know where we are. I lost track of the trail when we were looking at that sign, and then when I realized I was lost, I thought I knew the way back to the truck. But all these little pine trees got me turned around, and I think we need to pray and ask God to help us get back to the truck before dark."

In that moment, I felt a rare combination of panic and peace. I was frightened at the thought of being alone in those big woods after dark, at only ten years old, with the possibility of being eaten alive by any number of wild animals that lurked in the shadows (never mind that there were actually no carnivores of any size there, unless there was a random rabid squirrel that wanted to take us on). But alongside the sense of panic was a quiet, subtle sense of peace. I was not alone. I was with my daddy. Everything was going to be all right if I was with him. I remember how fast and hard my heart was beating. I also remember thinking that Daddy would get us out of there just fine, even though he admitted he was lost. I trusted his character and his ability regardless of our surroundings, the same way we must learn to trust God regardless of our circumstances.

Over and over in my adult life, I revisit that experience with my daddy in those woods. I continually feel those two conflicting emotions at the exact same moment. I panic at the least little things. When our checking account gets low, when the transmission falls out of my truck, or when one of my boys gets a headache, I immediately fall to pieces inside, assuming the worst possible scenario. But I also know we will somehow have enough money this month to pay the bills, that the transmission will not cost as much as I thought it would, and

> Fear may not go away, but it is trumped by faith in the God who loves you and cares for your every need.

that the small headache is not a brain tumor, it is just a kid that needs to go to bed a bit earlier. And though it seems impossible that fear and faith can dwell in the same vessel at the same time and take up the same space, they co-exist all the time. They must. It is not faith on my part at all if I don't choose to believe in the midst of fear and uncertainty.

And I return in my mind to the woods that afternoon, in the Sumter National Forest, with my daddy. A part of me thought we would die in those woods, but another part of me, a bigger and more rational side, knew we would be home in no time eating supper with Mama and telling stories about our day together.

I think we have gotten the idea of "faith" all wrong. Faith does not mean the absence of fear. Faith actually means choosing to trust in the midst of fear. It is admitting your fear and forging ahead toward an uncertain outcome, believing all the while that things will turn out right. God brings peace in the moment of panic seemingly out of nowhere—out of a dark and quiet corner of your heart you have not heard from in a while. But right there, just in time, when you need it most, while the sky is falling and the bills keep coming and dark clouds keep gathering, peace comes. Faith wins out. Fear may not go away, but it is trumped by faith in the God who loves you and cares for your every need.

We made it out of the woods right at dark. I had started to cry, I was breathing hard, and my heart was racing, when Daddy said, "The road ought to be up here in just a minute." I was too consumed with fear and panic to even watch where we were going until I followed Daddy through the bushes and stepped off the bank down onto the gravel road. Within a few minutes, we were sitting side by side in his black Ford pickup truck with the engine running and the heat roaring, thanking God for getting us back to the truck, and looking forward to what Mama would have ready for supper when we got home.

And we did make it home, to a big pot of chili and a warm fire in the stove. And you will make it home one day too. There will be a great feast waiting for you, the table will be set, and panic will give way to a peace that cannot be described—it can only be experienced. It is then, at home and safe, that we will wonder why we ever doubted.

CHAPTER 11

God in the Darkness

The Bible is replete with what I call "a theology of paradoxes." Time after time, the Scriptures will juxtapose two completely contradictory concepts that can't possibly make sense, we think, but upon further investigation and exploration, insight and understanding are gained and we see that the Bible does make sense after all. Consider this "passage of paradoxes" written by the apostle Paul to his friends at the church in the Greek city of Corinth, especially his comment about dying and living.

> *... Through glory and dishonor, bad report and good report; genuine, yet regarded as impostors; known, yet regarded as unknown; dying, and yet we live on; beaten, and yet not killed; sorrowful, yet always rejoicing; poor, yet making many rich; having nothing, and yet possessing everything* (2 Corinthians 6:8-10).

It seems as if Paul had stumbled upon something remarkable. He had concluded that the things the world placed value on were, in the end, superficial and unsatisfying. Yet he is not content to simply argue that these things (riches, wealth, comfort, prestige) were insufficient to bring life. He actually says that the opposites of these aspirations bring life, and the very things everyone labors for bring death if pursued apart from the gospel. At first glance, it is utter nonsense. Yet again, upon further investigation, the Christian who has applied this principle of doing things backward from the world's perspective will testify to the truth of this paradoxical idea—that we find life in hardships, trials, and the lowest places in our lives so long as we look to Jesus in those low places as our guide, companion, and friend.

I had just begun to explore the concept of being first in God's eyes by intentionally going last (or at least giving the whole "going last" thing my best shot) in my late teens. I admit, the idea of life coming from death sounded absurd until I began to ask the Holy Spirit to reveal how this would work in my own life. That was a stupid prayer. I may not have meant what I said, but God thought I meant it and He began to answer that prayer almost immediately.

(This may be a good time to drop in a helpful hint, dear friend. May I suggest that you carefully pray your prayers? God is way more serious about what we pray for sometimes than we are. So when you pray things like "Lord, break me," or "Lord, humble me," or the very worst and most dangerous of all prayers, "Lord, I will go anywhere and do anything for You, so do whatever it takes to get me ready," then you are inviting the hurricane of God's mysterious and effective action in your life. All I can say is, good luck…and keep a journal, 'cause things are about to get crazy.)

I prayed some of these prayers, or at least various combinations of them, because it seemed like I should. Wasn't it the right thing to ask God to remove my ego and destroy my pride and assassinate my sense of self-reliance? Oh, and while He was under the hood doing some soul maintenance, maybe He could do away with my anger and bitterness as well as annihilating my need to be seen, affirmed, applauded, recognized, and honored.

Evidently I was moving forward under the false and naive assumption that God would do all of this from outer space by osmosis. I thought He would just *think* all of that away for me, and *poof*—it would be gone! I didn't really think He would have to get right up close and lay His hands on me, hard, where it hurt the most. I wasn't ready for the bottom to fall out of my young life, but that is exactly what began to transpire. I hit a low place, and unbelievably, found life there.

Things began to go wrong on multiple levels. I mean falling apart! At age 18, I had already been preaching for four years and was living like it was an ironclad guarantee that God was going to bless everything I did from here on out because I had never been drunk or smoked weed or had sex with a girl. I had also sworn off R-rated movies and most secular, non-Christian music. So God owed me, big time. Then I had to go and pray that stupid prayer.

"God, break me. Show me what You meant when You said I could find life by losing it. Reveal to me what it means for the first to be last and the last to be first. Do whatever it takes, Lord. Just break me."

It was as if that itty-bitty prayer unleashed the wrath and fury of a thousand earthquakes right inside my little insignificant, innocent life. And in case you missed it, I was just 18.

The first thing that happened had to do with my father and his business. After nearly 40 years, my dad's electric-motor repair shop essentially went broke. And right around Christmas of that year, things got so bad that he had to start laying off employees. Within a few weeks he had shut the doors, unsure if they would ever open up again for business. My dad had also suffered a myriad of health problems over the years and it seemed as if this episode of bad luck with his business had really put him over the edge. He got really sick and lost his eyesight for several weeks. We later found out this was the beginning of his battle with diabetes.

On the heels of the business closing came my mom's stroke. I am certain that the stress of seeing my dad so discouraged, and the worry about how our family would survive, led to the stroke that nearly took her life. I remember taking her to the doctor myself that night. The physician spoke in disbelief after his second attempt to take her blood pressure, telling her that the upper number was over 300 and she should have died hours earlier. Her face began to draw down and the entire right side of her body went numb. Needless to say, I wasn't really feeling God too much about this time. It never occurred to me that all of these things could be the tools He was using to answer my sincere but naive prayer...you know, the one where I asked Him to do whatever it took to break me.

Finally, I had hoped that the Christmas holidays would be the time when my lifelong dream of going to college to play football would become a reality, at least on paper, since I would choose what school to play for during the break. I was a decent athlete who could learn offensive and defensive schemes fast. As a result of playing three years on varsity and knowing what to do on both sides of the ball, a handful of small colleges had shown an interest in me as a recruit. Though there was a good chance I would get some playing time fairly early at any of the smaller schools, I knew if I chose a bigger college, I would be lucky to ever see game time even as a senior. So I had resigned myself to picking a small school, preferably a Christian college where I could major in ministry while knocking heads on the field and eventually graduate prepared for a life of preaching the gospel. And there were even some schools offering very lucrative incentives in the form of football and academic combination scholarships. Bottom line? I was banking on football to get me to, and through, college.

That was until the end of our season. A stubborn will and a fear of asking to be taken out of the game effectively ended my chances at leaving our small town and getting an education on the football team's bill. I separated my shoulder in nine out of eleven games that year. I had learned how to grab it and pull it back in during the huddle before the next play. I was so afraid that if a scout found out I had a bad shoulder, they would quit calling and scratch me off their recruiting list. So I just sucked it up and kept playing. Ice and Advil were always there for me after the game, but they couldn't fix what I was doing to myself.

The pain increased, and after the season ended I would wake up and my entire arm would be numb from the shoulder to the fingers. After many tests I was told that the nerve damage was significant and that one good hit from a college linebacker could shred my shoulder joint. I needed surgery—to the tune of over $35,000. (This was 1991, and we had no insurance to cover it.) None of the scholarships were worth that much, and my athletic trainer strongly discouraged me from pursuing college football without surgery, rehab, and redshirting my freshman year.

When the letters and phone calls were returned informing the colleges of my injury, the correspondence dried up. In the words of one very diplomatic coach, they had to "leverage the possible risk against the potential reward" of signing a lineman/linebacker with a bad shoulder. Another was a bit blunter when he said, "You're damaged goods, and most schools wouldn't touch you now with a ten-foot pole."

I went from a hero to a zero in a matter of weeks. My future vanished away like the mist. My dad's lifework was all but gone, and my mother couldn't talk without slurring her speech. It was Christmas, and I hadn't even pursued college admittance apart from football as my ticket in. Panic ensued. Inside of me, my heart was filled with weeping, wailing, and gnashing of teeth. I slept very little and experienced worry for the first time. It just seemed like God had abandoned me. I simply couldn't comprehend that all of these very bad things were being used by a sovereign God to show me who He was and who I was, and that my hope and trust had been in the wrong things. He was doing what I had asked Him to do. I just forgot I had asked for it. I was in darkness. He was there with me, I would soon see.

One evening during this season of despair, I hit my lowest point emotionally. I was upstairs. The room was completely dark. As I lay on my back in bed, the tears had pooled up in my eyes and were hot on my skin. I was rehearsing my good deeds before God and feeling more and more rotten by the second as I tried to convince Him that, based on all my superior goodness, He should heal my mom, re-open Daddy's shop, and get me a full ride to Furman, Wake Forest, or Gardner-Webb. It was not working at all. God wasn't buying it. Neither was I.

It was then, out of the blue, as it were, that the very Holy Spirit of God came and stood on my chest. Hard. Right there in the darkness.

As if someone had snatched back dark curtains to reveal that it was noon outside and the sun was shining bright when I thought it was still 3 a.m. and dark, the light cascaded into my mind and my soul. The epiphany was tangible. It was like I could feel the light from the sun on my face, or maybe like I had been doused with a bucket of ice water unexpectedly while my head was turned the other way. What God unveiled to me right then and right there, with pools of hot tears in my eye sockets, took my breath away.

Son, I know you are lonely and afraid and confused. But I have not left you. I am simply doing what you asked Me to do and I am using these things to do it. I am breaking you and humbling you to prepare you for what lies ahead and to remind you to trust in Me alone. So trust Me. Not yourself. Not your plans. Not football. Not money. Not scholarships. Just trust Me.

It was His word for me. It struck deep and hit flesh. I was undone. I rolled out from under the covers and straight to my knees without even standing up. I just started weeping. It flooded me all at once. It was going to work out, somehow. God would prove trustworthy and I would be surprised by His plan. I could trust Him in the middle of all the unknown outcomes and uncertainties.

> Superficial circumstances had stayed static. It was the presence of God that was dynamic!

He was my hope and redeemer. Not my mom's health. Not the stability of my dad's business. Not even a college football scholarship. I had placed my faith everywhere but in the hands of the living God. I felt released from a stranglehold of fear and sadness.

I felt alive. I had to die to my own dreams to feel that life rise up in me.

But nothing had changed. All the circumstances were just as they had been five minutes earlier before I hit my knees. My dad's business was still closed. My mom's face still suffered from paralysis. My shoulder still hurt, and the schools still were not calling me anymore. Superficial circumstances had stayed static. It was the presence of God that was dynamic! He was moving on me and in me and I had been brought back to life in the midst of all that turmoil. In the middle of the darkness.

Not Alone

The crazy, backward way that God does things is meant to make no sense. It's not supposed to be predictable. So the more unlikely it is that you will be able to fix your problem, the more likely that God will come visit you in your darkness and save the day. It seems like He specializes in waiting for us to learn to wait on Him because we really don't have a choice. I mean, if God delays, we sort of have to wait. The question is not "Will you wait?" You have to. Case closed. The question is *"How* will you wait?" Will you wait grudgingly, or in earnest anticipation, or with your fists balled up and teeth clenched, or with carefree trust that He is always right on time?

So I ask you, what is your darkness right now?

Are you depressed? Is your mind constantly racing through worst-case scenarios? Have you just lost someone you cared for, either in death or a breakup? Are you broke, worried about money, behind on the bills, or ignoring the collection calls? Do you have a sick family member you can't fix? Is God ignoring some of your prayers? Are you addicted to something, and the shame is eating you alive? Are you still rehearsing and remembering hurtful words spoken to you years ago? Are you holding a grudge and looking for a chance to settle the score?

Give your darkness a name. Call it what it is. Because there is a very good chance you have an appointment with God there, and He wants to meet you right in the middle of the very thing that hurts you the most to show you that He will use it to break you. Not for the sake of your being broken. But for the sake of your seeing Him more clearly in your brokenness. For the sake of running to His grace in your brokenness. For the sake of worshipping Him for His providence and protection in your brokenness. For the sake of finding life by realizing you had not only lost it, you were never capable of handling it in the first place.

If you have not found yourself in real despair or darkness in a while, just wait. You will. And when you do, consider this insight into what God is doing in you during those seasons.

> If you are going through a personal trial now, there is a purpose in it, and the reason is more than just to develop you into a hardier person. It's true that God uses it to conform you to the image and character of Christ, and any trial is worth the pain for that process alone. But he aims also to show you the character of Christ in your trial.[10]

We are not competent enough or tough enough to handle the darkness and discouragement alone. So Christ meets us there with His tender mercies and tangible presence so we do not walk those valleys by ourselves. If the trials bring Him closer to us or make our awareness of His presence keener, then they serve a greater purpose and are worth the pain.

> Perhaps the revelation is only comfort for now and healing later. Perhaps it's healing and comfort now, with a visible display of God's miraculous power. Perhaps it's something you will only be able to see looking back on it one day from an eternal perspective. His specific plan for your trial may differ from his specific plan for someone else's trial, but

there's an aspect of himself to be revealed in it. Trust him. That aspect is there. It's always there.[11]

⚜

May God come to you in your darkest moments and show you the divine joy of being pulled from the pit of despair and being placed on the firm foundation of Christ Jesus. May you experience the cascading, brilliant light of God's presence in your darkest times. If you are dying to live, call out to God in the midst of your low point, your discouragement and depression and disappointment. He will meet you there.

He is God. Even when it's dark.

CHAPTER 12

Suffering for a Purpose

*It has been granted to you on behalf of Christ not
only to believe on him, but to also suffer for him.*

—PHILIPPIANS 1:29

OFTEN WHEN I PREACH THE GOSPEL, I spend time talking about
the necessity of the death of Christ on the cross and how the shed-
ding of His blood (His death) was necessary to insure the freedom and
salvation we now enjoy (our life). *Dying to Live* is more than a clever
book title. It also describes what Jesus did on our behalf. He died so
we might live.

A young man challenged me on this once after a sermon I preached
at his church. He simply could not understand how the blood of Jesus
shed through His suffering did anything at all for those of us living
2000 years later. I asked him to consider a different historical event to
get a better idea of how it worked. We began with the Revolutionary
War, where patriots shed their blood to gain our freedom from Brit-
ish tyranny. We moved on to the Civil War, where soldiers shed their
blood to keep the United States together and, eventually, give freedom
to black American slaves and all those that would be born from that
point forward. We ended by discussing World War II and the brave

soldiers from America and all over Europe who bled and suffered to stop Hitler's quest to rule the world despotically. The blood that was spilled represented the lives that were sacrificed as well as those that would be saved through the deaths of millions of heroes, from Normandy to Bull Run, from Appomattox to Iwo Jima. The life we enjoy now was bought with a great price: the blood and suffering of millions of people we've never even met. They all suffered for a purpose, and we gain life from their death.

Suffering for a purpose pays off. A greater purpose makes suffering worth it. Jesus suffered for a purpose: for God's glory and our redemption. Suffering is redemptive only if there is a greater purpose in view.

✤

I have met some interesting people on the road. You can buy my other books to read all about them. But it seems I am particularly drawn to people who have served in the military. I have never been in the armed forces, but my grandfather was a World War II veteran, and I believe I have always had a fascination with the military because of the stories he would occasionally tell us about his experience fighting the Japanese in the South Pacific.

When I meet people who have served in the military, I am always impressed at the dedication that is demanded of them, whether it's the time they spend away from their families or the physical and mental training they are subjected to or the atrocities they see with their own eyes on the battlefield. I have great respect and admiration for their sacrifice, though I myself have never felt compelled to serve in that capacity. (But I do admit that I secretly dream of running covert operations behind enemy lines. I always visualize myself as Jack Bauer from *24* meets Ethan Hunt from *Mission: Impossible,* rescuing civilians while dodging bullets from terrorists.)

> I...am always awestruck in their presence. They embody the idea of suffering for a purpose.

At the apex of my fascination with all things military is an elite force of men called Navy SEALs. These are the boys you don't mess with. They are the stuff of legends and movies. Perhaps the most highly skilled and specifically trained group of operatives on the planet, these warriors are good at everything from electronics to explosives. There are only 2600 of them on earth, according to the Pentagon. In my mind, they are a cross between ninjas and Jedi masters, like Yoda meets MacGyver. I have met a few in my day and am always awestruck in their presence. They embody the idea of suffering for a purpose.

In April of 2009, an elite team of SEAL snipers stole the international headlines by rescuing an American hostage from Somali pirates who had taken over his ship. This daring rescue further elevated their mystique and enhanced their reputation as the most highly trained and most feared elite military force on earth.

> Navy SEAL snipers endured some of the military's most rigorous training to enable them to carry out missions such as killing three Somali pirates holding a U.S. hostage with three precise shots Sunday. The making of a SEAL sniper involves more than three years of training, and that's only if the SEAL survives a process that culls three of four volunteers.[12]

According to a retired Navy SEAL I spent a few hours with once, this kind of heroic rescue is common, though not always reported in the news. Mere mortals like you and me are just not cut out for the kind of life the SEAL live or the suffering they must endure. I cringed when he told me what they were forced to endure in their training.

They go days without sleep. Their instructors know that the human body will eventually die without rest, and they push them right up to that limit. They will let them sleep for an hour after 48 hours of training, and then wake them up with a simulated enemy attack, thrusting them right back into a life-or-death situation, where they are forced to think with a sleep-deprived brain. This teaches them to react according to their training instead of thinking about a situation.

They spend hours and hours in freezing water. They have to tread water in high seas and swim for miles. Their trainers purposely capsize their boats to teach them how to survive in full body armor in the ocean until help arrives. They get them to the point of complete hypothermia and drill them with complicated questions about ammunition and firearms, or about offensive maneuvers against enemy combatants in the dark. Then they pull them out of the water, warm them up, and throw them back in. Repeat.

The man told me they would deny this, but he claimed he was locked in a casket and buried alive, underground, where he remained for 24 hours with no food, water, light, or movement. This exercise in mental suffering was designed to make him tough, to teach him to discipline his mind and the thoughts he was thinking when death seemed imminent and rescue unlikely. It also forced his mind to exercise authority over his body by telling his muscles not to cramp and his heart rate not to jump, avoiding the onset of panic, which would bring on hyperventilation and possibly even cardiac arrest.

The candidates were taken to remote areas in extreme heat, given compasses and coordinates, and told they had to make it to a rendezvous point in a few hours. Live ammo was fired over their heads, and their trainers fired mortars near them. Given no water, they became dehydrated and disoriented. If they failed to find their destination, they were forced to repeat the exercise.

They were made to run miles and miles with heavy packs in the rain, sometimes barefoot. They had to carry each other through harsh terrain to prepare for rescue missions. They had to assemble firearms and explosive devices while blindfolded in utter darkness as water was shot at them from a fire hose, to teach them to focus on important tasks in the midst of confusion and adversity.

The final challenge came when each recruit was thrown into frigid water, held under by the other recruits, and drowned when their lungs filled with water. Then it was the job of the rest of the team to revive and resuscitate the recruit. To join this elite unit, you had to literally die and be brought back to life.

Two things became clear to me during my conversation with this unique man. First, I was not cut out or called to be a Navy SEAL. Second, the only reason men are willing to submit themselves to such unthinkable torture is for something greater and nobler than themselves. They had to believe that all the suffering they endured was for a bigger purpose and would eventually affect more people than just themselves. They were willing to lose their lives so others could keep theirs.

This man had suffered. He even showed me scars. (I asked if he had any. He did.) But he suffered for a reason. There was a purpose to all the pain. He was doing it so he, of all people, could protect innocent people from evil forces, and so he could learn to go into impossible places and rescue hostages no one else on earth could possibly rescue.

For a moment, I felt small and insignificant next to this soldier who could kill me in literally 28 different ways, but could also have me airlifted out of an al-Qaeda bunker while blowing the place up with C-4. I had so many questions for him! I only asked a few, and this one that follows, along with his profound answer, gives another perspective on how we can actually find meaning and purpose in life by losing it and giving it away to something, or someone, greater than us.

I asked, "So what got you through all of the pain and torture? How did you keep from losing your mind? I would have quit, right on the spot, and gone home, but you stuck it out. Why? How?"

Without even a moment of hesitation, he said, "Oh, that's an easy question. When you go through what we went through, you have to hold on to something. You need an emotional anchor. For some guys it's their family, but since I wasn't married at the time, I just thought about all the American citizens I would have the chance to save. I mean, things happen in this world that we never know about, and there are some bad things that go down. Innocent people get killed, taken hostage, beaten and locked up for decades, and they eventually die without anyone ever knowing where they are or what happened to them. I wanted to be that guy who could go in and get 'em, bring 'em out alive, and get 'em home to their families safe and sound. That was my anchor. Knowing that if I didn't give up, one day I would be the guy who could get them out and get them home."

I replied, "So basically, you gave up everything to be a SEAL. You gave up all your childhood dreams, a college education, and the chance to make money, all for the chance to be an elite soldier in the Navy. You gave up your life for that."

His reply was priceless.

"Man, I didn't give up my life, I *gained* my life! I didn't sacrifice anything. I was blessed to be able to live my life to save the lives of others! That's what I was born to do."

The Greater Purpose

Isn't that not what we were born to do? As disciples of Jesus Christ, are we not born again by the Holy Spirit so we can live our lives as witnesses of the power of the gospel, saving others from pointless lives of selfish pursuits? A Navy SEAL found his purpose in life by laying aside all aspirations of selfish gain and dedicating himself to suffering for a greater good.

The Christian life is no different. In dying to myself, I suffer the pangs of withdrawal from materialism and convenience. I suffer the lack of sleep that comes from a late-night phone call when a friend has lost his mother to cancer and needs prayer. I suffer the physical and emotional stresses of embodying the hurts and struggles of those I minister to, pray for, and listen to. I empathize with a parishioner who has watched her father die slowly from the disease that ravages his body. I kneel and pray with siblings who wrestle with whether or not to place their mother in a retirement facility because of the horrors of Alzheimer's, which make it impossible for her to live alone anymore.

But in the long run, can I really call these things suffering? At the end of the day, have I actually sacrificed anything, other than the time and effort I would otherwise have expended on my own dead-end pursuit of worldly happiness? This is what I was born to do. This is what the Christian was born again to do! To come alive in times of need, crisis, suffering, and loss, and to come to the aid and help of those in need as God's ambassadors of grace and mercy. When I labor in the hope that a greater purpose is being accomplished and I am a small part of that greater purpose, I am forced to realize that I have not ever really suffered or sacrificed.

God evidently wants to employ us in His purposes, using us as His ambassadors, rescuers, encouragers, authors, preachers, mothers and fathers, counselors, and friends. Once we accept the responsibility He places on us, it's certain that hard times await us. Suffering will come. And when I am in middle of a valley of discouragement, it certainly feels like I'm suffering. No one can tell you otherwise when you are in the throes of pain (even when you are on a mission as God's ambassador of peace and reconciliation). But once we escape that moment of inconvenience and hurt, we gain a better perspective, and looking back on the painful experience, we see that the end result was worth what we suffered.

> The endgame for the Christian is that we might find life by recognizing we are not the center of the universe.

A mother watches her son walk across the stage at his high-school graduation. She beams with pride! She does not remember the pain of giving birth to her son at that moment. She is caught up in the glory of his great accomplishment.

A father walks his daughter down the aisle at her wedding and sees her face light up when her eyes meet the groom's. He does not remember the sleepless nights when she had colic as an infant at that moment. He is caught up in the glory of his lovely daughter, who is about to be married.

A college football team wins a national championship on national television and everyone celebrates. Not a single player is thinking about the heat, humidity, or muscle cramps he felt during the first week of practice in July at that moment. They are caught up in the glory of a great victory.

A pastor watches a wife and husband embrace in tears on the couch in his study. After weeks of counseling, they have decided to make their marriage work and stop talking about divorce. That pastor is not remembering the late-night cram sessions before a seminary exam in pastoral care and counseling at that moment. He is caught up in the glory of a saved relationship.

When we *suffer* for a purpose, we eventually *see* that greater purpose. Even if we only see glimpses of it, the glory of that purpose (the wedding, the graduation, the championship ring, the saved marriage) overshadows and dwarfs whatever sacrifices we made to get there. Glory trumps suffering, but only if there is a purpose to it, a goal, an endgame. The endgame for the Christian is that we might find life by recognizing we are not the center of the universe. We simply live for and serve the One who is.

🦃

The call of discipleship is a call to suffer, but the suffering is not random or meaningless. There is a greater purpose on the horizon and the results belong to God. In suffering we embrace the idea of dying to our desires of convenience and safety in order to come alive to the presence of God's kingdom, here and now, advancing with love and mercy and power.

Each time we suffer, if we will submit ourselves to God in the midst of the struggle, a little more of our old self will die, along with its selfishness and sin, and the life of Christ will slowly take its place. It allows us to die some more so we might become more alive. But only if it is for that purpose—the purpose of dying to live.

Therefore we do not lose heart. Though outwardly we are wasting away, yet inwardly we are being renewed day by day. For our light and momentary troubles are achieving for us an eternal glory that far outweighs them all. So we fix our eyes not on what is seen, but on what is unseen. For what is seen is temporary, but what is unseen is eternal (2 Corinthians 4:16-18).

CHAPTER 13

My First Real Run

Since we are surrounded by such a great cloud of witnesses, let us throw off everything that hinders and the sin that so easily entangles, and let us run with perseverance the race marked out for us.

—HEBREWS 12:1

HAVE YOU EVER TRIED SOMETHING that you absolutely hated the first time you did it, only to find yourself doing it over and over again and asking yourself why, since you hated it so much in the beginning?

Hot sauce, for example. Why would a sane person willingly subject themselves to placing a food item inside their mouth that makes them cry, sweat, cough, gag, and get hiccups? I don't have an answer. Yet I am among the elite few who douse everything from salads to chicken and dumplings with Tabasco or Texas Pete. It still hurts my mouth and I still crave it.

In considering the paradox of dying to live, we have to ask ourselves how in the world we end up loving something, someone, that can cause us so much suffering and grief. How is it possible to love following Jesus as a true disciple, when so much of the Christian life involves fighting against the world? Going against the trends? Being misunderstood, ridiculed, mocked? Living life backward, putting others first, serving instead of being served? Is it possible to actually enjoy this kind of life? It seems impossible that I would relish and savor living my life in last place while everyone else takes the coveted spot in the front of the line.

I contend that it is indeed possible to love this kind of life that runs against the grain of human nature. I would go further and say that it is not only possible, it is expected! We can indeed love something that is right and noble and good for us, even if it causes us pain and grief at times.

Consider the sport of running. For me, this proves you can enjoy and savor something painful. My first real experience running for fun was not fun. It was horrible, excruciating, and embarrassing. It happened my freshman year in college.

☙

College. The mention of the word can inspire a thousand different images and just as many different memories.

Lots of people hark back to their college days. Some of them recall favorite professors, most difficult classes, and all-nighters finishing a paper. Many more wish they could have it back: little responsibility, afternoon naps, a metabolism that still worked, and a figure that was 30 pounds lighter.

Sit in on any conversation among college graduates or dropouts, and sooner or later the subject matter turns to "my most miserable college experience." One recalls a crazy ex, another tells with surprising clarity all that he did while unconsciously drunk, while still another admits he never once changed his bedsheets or pillowcase. In four years. Gross.

Mine was the first time I went running.

It's not entirely true for me to say that this was my first running experience. Because like most kids, I ran all the time from age two onward, but never in an organized fashion, and certainly never for the sheer fun of it. Running in short spurts while playing army in the woods was fun. Running at recess was fun. But the only other kind of running I did before college was forced upon me. Compulsory running. Handed down as punishment for missing a tackle or slung upon me as conditioning, to work me into shape for the season. Coaches made us run sprints, laps, suicides, and circles. I hated running when I was made to run. I vaguely remembered enjoying it as a little boy in the woods and on the playground.

Maybe it was the echo of those memories that instigated my most miserable college experience.

Actually, it was a combination of things. I was an 18-year-old invincible freshman. I was at college, and running is what college students were supposed to do. And—a big group of upperclassmen, all of whom I desired to impress, were talking about it in the cafeteria one day at lunch. Fatefully, I overheard them talking. It was my chance to impress the big boys.

It was about 15 minutes until my daily nap, but they were going to run. And they talked about it as if it were the sole purpose for which God had put humans on the globe. Within five minutes of eavesdropping from the next table, not only was I convinced I had to run with them, I was also sure that running would cure cancer, end world hunger, and stop the polar ice caps from melting. Plus I would be initiated into their way-cool guy club by making a lap around campus with them. It was a two-mile loop. How hard could that be?

I had played baseball, football, and basketball in high school. I was not overweight. I drank a glass of water once or twice a week, so I was hydrated. We would meet outside of Lutz Dorm at 1:30. I finished my taco pie, cheese fries, Mountain Dew, and ice-cream cone, then headed back to my dorm to prep for our mini-marathon.

This was about to go completely wrong. I had never been so stupid and ignorant about any one thing in my short life.

No stretching. No warming up. No running shoes. No time to digest my carbohydrate grease feast from lunch.

I was wearing Nike high-top basketball shoes when they came to get me. There were about eight of them. All skinny and fit. Wearing Asics Gels and ankle socks. Juniors and seniors, they were. And I, a mere freshman, who knew more about the history of Viking sword-smithing than running.

It was a chilly, overcast day with a thick mist in the air, and as soon as we had made it out of the parking lot, I knew I was doomed. These guys were professionals. They were running really fast. I would never be able to keep up with them at the pace they set. My lungs immediately filled with molten lava. My throat was about to rupture. Long strands of mucus began to form and then hung from my nostrils, and massive amounts of phlegm kept crawling up my windpipe. Death was near. I would soon meet the Lord.

But the one thing I could not afford to do was admit my unpreparedness. Death would be better than embarrassment. So I pressed on. We had covered about 200 yards.

At about 300 yards, my legs atrophied. The muscles froze and my shins and calves turned to stone. My right side felt like a coal furnace and my left side like a habañero pepper farm. I remember thinking I had fallen into the burning ring of fire that Johnny Cash sang about.

I swore to myself and promised God that if I made it back to my dorm, I would NEVER EVER run again unless bad guys with weapons were chasing me, or wild animals with rabies and leprosy. These guys were nuts if they enjoyed this. They must have all been trying to impress each other too, for that was the only possible motivation on earth to make eight other young men voluntarily undergo such unspeakable torture.

On the backside of the campus, about three-quarters of the way around the two-mile loop, was a hill that stretched straight up for about 400 yards. It was the very first thing I thought about when my lungs and throat began to fill with battery acid, but I knew I would have to face it eventually, and ascend it. Walking back was not possible.

Up to "the hill" I had managed to stay within sight distance of the pack, though in last place. I did this by sheer will and toughness. At such a young age, I could absorb abuse for a season. But when we started up "the hill" they simply pulled away. Like LeBron James playing basketball with a bunch of eighth-graders, they were a different breed than me. I was running. They were runners.

Sucking in air like a Hummer sucks fossil fuels, I limped to the top of the hill, but they were out of sight when I got there. They did not wait. In a weird mixture of shame for being so slow and weak, and accomplishment for having made it without stopping (or throwing up), I caught that famous "second wind" every runner understands. And by the time I got back to the dorm, my legs were hot as fire and my skin was stinging and tingling. My breathing had slowed down and my head had quit throbbing.

I arrived in the parking lot of my dorm like a victorious quarterback arrives for the hometown parade after winning the Super Bowl. The transformation was intense. Just a mile earlier I had sworn off this nonsense for life. But now that I had completed the loop and pushed through the pain, proving to myself that I was capable of more than I had anticipated, a rush of accomplishment swept over me. It could have been the adrenaline or the endorphins, but I felt cleaned out and purified. The rest of that day I felt unusually good all the way around. My heart rate had reached its peak. My muscles were sore and my joints stiff. But oh man, did I feel awesome!

I broke my promise. The one I made to myself and to God. The one where I said I would never run again.

I have been running ever since that day. Not every day, but consistently. And even when I go through seasons where I can't keep to a regimen, running always calls me back. Every day I think about it. Every other day I try to do it. From the inaugural two-mile loop of anguish, I was hooked. Something so miserable and painful became my escape.

Running is good for me, even though it hurts. It is a big part of my life. It burns calories. It releases endorphins. It builds muscle and burns fat. It keeps me physically fit. It keeps me emotionally balanced. It allows my mind space to breathe and think. It exposes me to fresh air, sunshine (and in turn vitamin D), and it gives me a release from the stresses and anxieties I carry around in my neck and shoulders. It relaxes me, helps me rest at night, makes me a more patient father and husband, and hopefully is increasing my life span.

> The longer I run, and the longer I follow Jesus, the more joy I find in the experience...The more I suffer, the more I enjoy the relationship.

Who knew something so painful and unenjoyable would one day become one of my greatest passions?

There are so many parallels to running and my relationship with Jesus, they are almost limitless. A few come to mind...

I was totally unprepared and naive going into my first run, just like I was when Christ saved me at age 14.

I did not have any of the right gear or equipment for either task when I first started.

I had no experience in either one and no idea what to expect.

I walked into both blind, naive, and cocky, but was quickly humbled by the reality of the challenge.

I quickly learned, in running and in my faith, to push through the pain and keep moving forward.

I noticed that my brothers drove me on and their very presence would not let me quit.

I took comfort in knowing that my friends had suffered, or were suffering, the same thing I was going through.

I knew the destination was fixed, so when I wanted to quit, I just had think about reaching it.

At first my desire was to impress others. Now my desire is to savor every moment as a treasure and a joy.

At first I feared the boys I ran with. Now the only thing I fear is the day when I will be too old to keep going.

At first I relied on my natural ability, which was useless. Now I rely on discipline, wisdom, and conditioning.

At first I needed to keep up with the others. Now I don't try to impress anyone, so I go at my own pace.

The longer I run, and the longer I follow Jesus, the more joy I find in the experience.

And as odd as it sounds, the suffering actually makes it mean more to me. The more I suffer, the more I enjoy the relationship.

Is it any wonder that the apostle Paul referred to running so often in the New Testament? "We run this race with patience that is set before us," he says. "Don't you know that in a race, all the runners compete for the prize?" he says. For a great number of people, the similarities are meaningless because they have never run. But you do not have to have the experience to understand the point.

Life is a marathon, not a sprint. And the best part about running the race of life as a Christian is that I always have a companion who knows more than I do and can run farther than me, but will always stay right with me to make sure I make it to the finish line.

So the struggles and pains and discouragements that come with following Jesus as His disciple actually serve to whet your appetite for Him. Just like I crave a good run now, even though it will make my muscles and joints ache, I crave intimacy with Christ, even though I know I will feel most intimate with Him when I am suffering for Him or serving someone in His name. It is quite a paradox, but it makes perfect sense, especially once you have tried it and found it to be true.

CHAPTER 14

Enduring Hardship with Two Little Witnesses

Endure hardship with us like a good soldier of Christ Jesus…
Remember Jesus Christ, raised from the dead, descended
from David. This is my gospel, for which I am suffering
even to the point of being chained like a criminal. But
God's word is not chained. Therefore I endure everything
for the sake of the elect, that they too may obtain the
salvation that is Christ Jesus, with eternal glory.

—2 TIMOTHY 2:3,8-10

SUFFERING IS GOD'S WAY OF BREAKING US. He uses it to humble us. To show us that we're not in charge. To force us to give up on being self-reliant and throw ourselves at His feet trusting His providence instead of our own. It is the tool He employs to cut out and kill the things in us that would eventually destroy us. The pride, the lust, the arrogance, the jealousy, the envy, the bitterness, the greed.

There is a purpose in suffering for believers who will see the hand of God at work in the darkest times of their lives. I remind myself during seasons of discouragement and hardship that God's way of doing things is backward, so whatever difficulty I'm facing is His way of doing something in me that can't be done any other way. When I feel like I'm losing, I'm actually winning. When I'm suffering, it is actually a blessing. God is using things like these in the lives of His children to purify and cleanse us and give us life as we die to all other loves and desires and He becomes preeminent.

Now, lots of things sound good in theory but don't really deliver in the real world where we live—you know, the one with bills and taxes and the flu.

Take a pill to help you lose weight. You will never, ever need to exercise or practice portion control. Eat all you want and get skinny. Sounds good. But it does not work. Ever!

Make an extra $35,000 a month in cash without ever leaving your house. Straight from your laptop. They even have commercials with real people on them to testify that the scam works. Too bad they are paid actors who are working a regular job like the rest of us.

Get out of debt. Tomorrow. No matter how much you owe. Never mind that you spend too much and are too lazy to show up to work so you always get fired. Just call a toll-free number and the bill collectors will magically quit calling.

To tell the truth, sometimes a good example is more effective than a good written argument or a great commercial. Certainly, hearing stories of people who overcome great obstacles inspires within us the faith that we too can move mountains.

But seeing someone do this firsthand carries even more of a lifelong impact. When we get the opportunity to watch someone endure the difficulties of marriage and yet manage to stay married, it gives us hope that we can make it too. When we see a family pull together to help a loved one battle cancer, we know we could do the same if we had to.

This book is a written argument that we find life by giving it away, by dying to our selfishness, as we are made alive by the power of the risen Christ. Fortunately, I had a real-life example who showed me how God's paradox of finding life by losing it really worked (I hope you also have some examples you can emulate). His name was Wilkes

Skinner. He was my pastor, mentor, and one of my heroes. But his life was not the kind anyone would ever want. At least not anyone with any common sense.

I want to ask Jesus when I get to heaven why some people just seem to get beaten down all their lives. Wilkes Skinner, at least in the years I knew him, just always seemed to be in the crosshairs of a major tragedy. And in my mind, this made no sense, because he was a preacher and God was supposed to take care of preachers. He had no idea that a little boy like me was watching him in those tragedies and paying attention to how he responded to them. He showed me how to find life by giving it away. He endured.

His oldest daughter was born with a mental handicap. Her physical, mental, and emotional development all stopped short and at a very early age, she was placed in an assisted-living facility for children with severe developmental issues who required round-the-clock specialized care and observation. Wilkes and his wife, Mary, would have rather raised her at home but simply could not risk the potential dangers. Yet they loved her and spent time with her consistently, and they never complained. I never once heard them ask why God allowed it to happen that way. They were faithful living examples of people who trusted God in the midst of severe family struggles.

Years later, Wilkes and Mary were on a ski trip one winter, when she fell on the slopes and broke her leg. The trip to the hospital for X-rays ended up uncovering a terrible disease that would have eventually taken her life. She had cancer of the bone marrow. The only hope for survival was a bone-marrow transplant. This long and painful procedure took over a year. She and Wilkes moved to the state of Washington and lived there for 12 months. Our church hired an interim pastor, and every Sunday morning, our congregation would listen to a short message played from a cassette tape that Wilkes had recorded and mailed across the country to our church. We would cry when his voice would come over the sound system.

Our church rallied around Wilkes and Mary and prayed. God

spared her life and she was able to eventually come home, but she battled a case of the shingles for many years after the transplant. She was in constant pain. Yet she never once complained. She still taught Sunday school and vacation Bible school and sang in the choir every Sunday. And she still continued to visit their daughter regularly at Whitten Village. Together, they continued to endure.

But perhaps the most tragic event to touch the life of this dear man of God and his family was the death of their youngest son. On a normal day, their little boy was playing in the yard when the unthinkable happened. He was run over by an automobile, and the family lost their precious child. It still gives me a lump in my throat when I imagine the dark days they went through as a family dealing with such an unimaginable sorrow.

I will never fully understand how Wilkes was able to continue in ministry after such unspeakable pain had gripped his soul. But maybe it was those very sorrows that God used in his life to make him the kind of caring shepherd the sheep needed. He served the church in the midst of death and loss and grief. He lived the life of Christ even while death raged around him. He had lost nearly all things for Christ yet possessed a peace and joy that magnified the glory of God. And as a pastor who cared for the souls of people, no one could ever accuse him of not understanding their loss, heartache, disappointment, or confusion. He had been where they had been.

He was able to speak life and give life because of the loss and death that had touched his own.

His endurance left an indelible mark on my soul as a very small boy. The tragedies were not secret, and neither was the pain and suffering that accompanied them. I can recall being amazed at his ability to preach on Sundays when his wife was so very sick at home. There was clearly an unseen power that both energized and sustained him in those dark and difficult days. He had entered into an intimate and personal place with Jesus Christ I am certain I have never been to, simply because he had so much in common with Jesus based on the sufferings they had shared. He had received grace from God to get him through days and nights I have never even dreamed of going through. He pastored and ministered out of his hurt, and the grace God sent him to heal those hurts. I had a front-row seat as a little boy to all of this. His endurance stuck with me.

At age 14, after a well-orchestrated plan by the Holy Spirit to bring me to my knees, I repented of my sin and trusted Christ. I immediately felt a call to ministry—and guess who was right there to encourage me? Of course, it was my pastor, Wilkes Skinner. The first message I ever preached was from his pulpit on March 27, 1987. He told me I had an open invitation to preach anytime I wanted at the church. He would sit with me after sermons and tell me what a good job I had done and offer me encouragement and ideas on how to make my sermons better and more effective. He possessed tenderness and gentle love that, looking back, I can tell came from the years of suffering and many sorrows he'd had to endure.

And a few years later, a boy I had grown up with also surrendered to the ministry in our church. Wilkes treated him the same way and gave him opportunities to preach. His name was Brian Burgess. We were childhood buddies. Now we are grown men and best friends. And our common denominator was the life and example of our suffering and faithful pastor.

❦

Now, over two decades later, Wilkes and his wife are very old and in poor health. He preached faithfully into his seventies until he couldn't do it anymore. Both are in the twilight of their lives. And they are facing death. The strange twist, however, is that their life and legacy will live on long after death has taken their bodies to the grave—at least in the lives of two little boys who saw their faithfulness.

Brian Burgess is faithfully teaching the Word and preaching the gospel to this day. He and his wife have three boys they are raising in the Christian faith to be young men of God. He has an amazing ministry to bikers and leads dozens of them to Christ every year. He has a ministry among the Navajo Indian nation in Arizona as well as a thriving ministry at his church. He has finished his master's degree and doctorate of ministry degree. He is one of the few men I know who has an effective ministry leading Muslims to faith in Christ. He is still one of my closest and most trusted friends, and he has been faithful to God's calling on his life since he was 16 years old and Wilkes Skinner took him under his wing and mentored him. He is modeling the endurance he saw exemplified in front of him.

> We asked each other what it was about Wilkes that made him so special and why he had such a deep impact on both of us.

I have preached in 30 countries and 45 states to several million people. Our camps have raised over $500,000 for missions since 1998. I preach on the radio and have written numerous books. I have seen over 60,000 people repent of their sins and trust Christ for salvation since 1987, to God be the glory.

And a few years ago, Brian and I were together in Athens, Greece, reflecting back on our lives and our callings and remembering the good old days as little boys running around the old church parking lot. As we stood on the Acropolis looking at Mars Hill, where Paul preached the gospel to the Athenians in the book of Acts, guess who we talked about?

Wilkes Skinner. The man who stood strong even when death raged around him. The pastor who preached a simple gospel message and backed it up by shepherding his flock with compassion. The man who opened his pulpit to two teenage boys and said we could preach anytime we had a message from God. We asked each other what it was about Wilkes that made him so special and why he had such a deep impact on both of us, even 20 years after we had both moved away and moved on in ministry.

The answer was clear. Without a doubt, it was the depth of suffering he had endured in life and his steadfast faithfulness in the face of all the unanswered questions, disappointments, and dark days. He had actually breathed life into us two young boys by being faithful in hard times. We came to the conclusion that our lives would have turned out quite differently if Wilkes's life had been different. We would never have had that example of quiet confidence in God if he had not endured all that pain and loss.

The things that man went through would have killed most people. Yet God in His sovereignty used every bit of it for another purpose, and now the example he showed Brian and me lives on in each sermon we preach, every person we lead to Christ, all the books we write, and how we train up our children. I am pretty sure that when Wilkes stands before the Lord, he will receive a crown of righteousness for his faithful, humble service in the midst of such great loss.

Long after Wilkes has died, his life will live on. We were watching him. He was faithful. Thank God for this witness.

> *We know that in all things God works for the good of those who love him, who have been called according to his purpose* (Romans 8:28).

CHAPTER 15

What If I Still Want to Be First?

I LOVE HONEST QUESTIONS, and the most honest ones almost always come from children or teenagers.

At our Crossroads summer camps, we host thousands of students from all over America every year. The first night during one of our camps, a young man was convicted by the Holy Spirit and repented of his sins and trusted Christ. Visibly moved by the gospel, he began his journey of faith and salvation.

He came to me Wednesday night at supper (two days later) and asked me simply, "I've been saved for a couple of days now and I was wondering…when do I quit sinning?"

Great question. It also comes in other forms.

When do I stop lusting?

When do I quit struggling with anger?

When do I totally forgive all the people who have hurt me?

How long before I stop cursing and lying?

When do I stop snapping my spouse's head off?

How long before I can control my appetite?

How long until I become patient with my children?

At what point do I naturally desire to let others in front of me in line?

When does it get easier to give large amounts of money to missions or the poor?

When do I stop comparing myself to other people?

When do I quit being envious of the houses and cars and salaries my friends have?

Questions like these only have one real answer. WHEN JESUS COMES BACK. Until we are made perfect and complete in Him, we will remain in the crucible of pain, walking the narrow and rocky road holding onto an unseen hand of grace, hoping that the life of Christ is growing in us as the old nature and its habits die a little bit more each step of the journey. Dying to live happens slowly as new life replaces the old, as we remain in the life-giving vine of Christ.

Since it is our nature to want to be first, best, biggest, and noticed, what happens if, after years of knowing and being known by Jesus, we find ourselves settling into old habits: jockeying for position, asserting our rights, and claiming our place at the front of the line? The short answer is…God will not give up on you. He owns you and He will keep working with your lump of clay until the useful vessel He desires emerges. Consider Paul's words to his friends in the city of Philippi as he encouraged them with a reminder of God's faithfulness to them.

> *I thank my God every time I remember you. In all my prayers for all of you, I always pray with joy because of your partnership in the gospel from the first day until now, being confident of this, that he who began a good work in you will carry it on to completion until the day of Christ Jesus* (Philippians 1:3-6).

Our hope when we slip back into old habits of selfishness, materialism, and competition is that we don't have to fight those battles on our own. There is a greater power at work in us and He is not going to bail out on what He has already begun. It is God's desire to complete what He started in us, to see it through and take glory in the finished project. I find myself down in the dumps when the old me comes roaring back to life and the same old feelings of insecurity or envy re-emerge.

I wonder how I could still be fighting those battles after so many years of following Jesus. Despair then begins to set in as I question my walk with Him, wondering if I have really made any progress or if I have backslidden in my relationship with Him.

Then the Holy Spirit reminds me of this truth and I take courage: I am not working on this by myself. As a matter of fact, this entire endeavor was not even my idea in the first place. It is God Himself who started the process of salvation and it is God Himself who will finish it. He has way too much invested to walk away when the stocks are down and the market looks gloomy.

> God gave His Son to be killed so we might live. Do you really think He would abandon His plan after pouring so much love and effort into it?

He is not in this for a short-term profit. He will stick with His investment and work on it internally and vigorously so the finished product will resemble His Son, Jesus Christ—because Jesus was His investment in us.

God gave His Son to be killed so we might live. Do you really think He would abandon His plan after pouring so much love and effort into it? We are His plan, and He won't walk away, even when we still want to be first and seem to fall back into our old ways. Dying to live means that we have to keep on dying. And dying. And dying some more. There are practical ways to approach this on a daily basis and to see life spring from death in your own life.

Practice What Jesus Preached

> *Jesus said to the crowds and to his disciples: "The teachers of the law and the Pharisees sit in Moses' seat. So you must obey them and do everything they tell you. But do not do what they do, for they do not practice what they preach"* (Matthew 23:1-3).

All this talk of dying to ourselves and embracing the life of sacrifice sounds cool as long as it's just words on a page. You can read all day long and even nod your head in agreement. You may even groan and moan, or go all the way and say "amen" as you underline and highlight powerful points and takeaways. But at some point, we actually must begin to apply what Jesus tells us to do. We have to stop reading about it and start doing it. We have to stop expecting everyone else to obey what Jesus said, and *we* need to start obeying it. And just because you give it a good effort doesn't mean it will happen overnight. You will still desire first place. You will still want to sit in the pilot's seat and control your own life. These things don't magically change with the wave of a wand. It takes time and major surgery by the Holy Spirit.

When Jesus was teaching the crowds in Matthew 23, He was addressing people who knew full well that the religious leaders who exercised authority over them were guilty of a great hypocrisy. Jesus even went so far as to chide them when He said, in essence, you can do what they say but not what they do. Don't follow their example because they waste their entire lives debating the meaning of the Scriptures, never placing their lives in subjection to its authority. So it was actually Jesus Himself who gave us that common phrase "practice what you preach." Except He actually did it. And He expects us to do the same.

This is how the paradoxical truth moves from theory to reality. This is how God proves that the last really do come first in the kingdom of God and that those who give their lives away really do find meaning and purpose.

It moves from theory to reality when WE ACTUALLY PUT IT INTO PRACTICE! When you decide to test it out yourself. When you start living like the words Jesus spoke were meant to be taken literally and applied in everyday life instead of taken figuratively and debated in a coffee shop over a latte. I find if I can distract myself by arguing about what Jesus really meant, then I never have to get around to actually doing what He said. Does this sound familiar to you? Until I actually obey Him I will never understand Him. We gain understanding when we obey. It is when we give up fighting Him, come under submission to His authority, and begin following His commands that the dark clouds of confusion clear and the bright sun of understanding dawns on us. Obedience is the big secret.

I would admonish you to do more than just read the words of Jesus. That alone is insufficient.

You also must go beyond simply hearing the stories and testimonies of those who have tested the commands of Christ and found them to be life-giving and exhilarating. This, too, is not enough.

You must take action, because action is the only cure for apathy and indifference.

The Cure for Your Apathy

Before my grandmother died, I recall hearing her say that the only way to stay healthy and mobile was to get up and keep moving. That was one of her favorite little quips. According to her, the very moment an old person decided to just sit around, they began to die. She said that if she ever stopped getting up and moving around, she would wind up in a wheelchair one day and six feet under the next.

Modern science and exercise physiology have proven this old wisdom true. It seems that motion and activity are indeed the keys to maintaining muscular strength, bone density, healthy blood flow, lower cholesterol levels, and prime brain function. When we move, the fibers and cells that make us human begin to labor and work, moving blood cells, creating oxygen, firing brain synapses, and sending and receiving millions of tiny impulses every moment. Brain specialists have discovered that rigorous and challenging brain activity can even delay the onset of Alzheimer's disease, because thinking hard and learning new ways of doing things force the neural pathways inside the human brain to stretch and strain,

> We have to get up and we have to move our faith. It's not faith at all, if all it ever does is sit and think and talk.

forging new routes and keeping blood flow active to the parts of the brain that would otherwise lie dormant due to non-use.

You may not find this as fascinating as I do, but I hope you see the similarities between how the human body works and how the human spirit works. We are, after all, called the body of Christ in Scripture. It takes work for a body to stay healthy and fight off disease and sickness. The same applies to our hearts, our spirits, the place inside of us where Christ has set up residence.

To put it simply, we must take action. We have to get up and we have to move our faith. It's not faith at all, if all it ever does is sit and think and talk. It becomes faith when it mobilizes in response to the commands of Jesus. He commands us to choose last place, to consider others better than ourselves, to love genuinely, and to serve consistently. All of these require action and movement and they result in not only finding life, but in the enjoyment of the life we have been graciously given by God. In the same way I experience rest and relaxation after a good six-mile run or a strenuous 60-minute workout, our spirits are renewed and refreshed when we exercise: when we exercise our hearts and minds in obedience to the call of discipleship, the command to assume the lowest position and give up the highest ones to others so God in His own way might exalt us in due season, so we in turn might give the highest place to Christ. There is more to the kingdom of God than taking the best seat at the banquet and being honored as the greatest person in the room. There is work to be done. We must move in obedience.

I read a story that illustrates this principle perfectly.

It seems that a woman with more money than she knew what to do with became extremely depressed. After weeks of battling the blues, she went to a counselor a friend had recommended to her. Though reluctant, she eventually went out of desperation because she could not shake the feeling that something was wrong deep down inside her soul.

She sat down with the counselor. He asked, "So tell me how you are feeling and what is going on inside you right now."

She responded, "Well, I just feel depressed all the time. There is a dark cloud that hangs over my head and I cannot escape it. I don't care about anything anymore and I just want to lie in bed all day long. I can't get motivated about anything—and I'm irritable and grumpy and I never rest well. I just feel a mess!"

The counselor was curious. "So tell me about your life, your job, your family, and what your average day is like."

Her response shocked him. "I don't have a job. I don't need one. I am rich beyond your wildest imagination and haven't had to worry about money since I was married. My husband has seen that I have everything I need or want. He works all the time and is never home. My children are all grown and have moved away. I'm lonely without them. I live in a huge house all by myself with no one to talk to. I just want to die sometimes. I know that is awful to say, but it's true! What in the world is wrong with me? I have enough money to buy anything I could ever want—but I'm miserable!"

The counselor was writing the entire time she was talking. He then folded up the piece of paper and handed it to her. "Do not read this until you arrive back at your house. When you open it, you must do *exactly* what it says, even if you don't think it will work. Promise me you will do *exactly* what it says!"

This sounded a bit strange so she asked, "Is this a prescription? If I could just find the right medicine to get my head straight, I know I would be fine."

"Oh yes, this is a prescription I feel certain will straighten things out for you in a few weeks. But you have to take it in *exactly* the way I tell you to, do you understand?" The counselor sounded very stern in his admonition that she follow his instructions exactly as he gave them. So she said yes and left his office, having thought that the visit would last a little longer.

All the way home she could barely stand it. She fought the urge to open the prescription, even though she couldn't imagine why he would make her wait to open it when she could easily stop by the drugstore on the way home and have the prescription filled. So when she arrived back at her big, empty house, she walked straight into the kitchen. She opened the paper to find these surprising words written.

This may sound odd to you, but I don't think you will find health in a pill. Your problem is easy to diagnose. You are lazy and bored. You have lived your life for yourself for so many years that you have amassed everything you ever wanted. But it has not brought you happiness. So here is your prescription. You must take it exactly *as I say or it will not make you better.*

Monday—Get up early and go to the assisted living facility closest to you. Tell them you are there to spend the day with their residents who never have any visitors. Talk to them, help clean their rooms, sing or play the piano, and eat with them. You must stay until dinner.

Tuesday—Go downtown to the soup kitchen and tell them you are there help distribute food during lunch. Tell them you will help cook it if they need you to, and stay and clean up after they are finished. Then ask them to make a list of all the groceries they need till the next Tuesday. Go to the store and buy everything on that list and bring it back.

Wednesday—Go to the hospital and ask to speak with the head chaplain. Tell him that you want to spend the day making rounds with him, learning people's names. Then when you feel confident enough, begin going from room to room and ask the patients if you can pray for them. Spend some time in there and visit with them. Stay until dinner.

Thursday—Go to your local Red Cross and tell them you have a good vehicle and want to spend the day delivering free meals to shut-ins who have no transportation. They will probably send someone with you who knows the route and knows who needs food that day. Don't come home until every meal has been delivered.

Friday—Call and speak with the principal at the local elementary school. Tell them you have a lot of time available and want to be a mentor for some of their students who are at risk and come from rough home situations. You can go read to some classes, you can be a lunch buddy and eat with some of the students, or you can even volunteer to head up a fundraiser to raise money for a new playground.

Saturday—Sleep as late as you want. Spend the day with your husband doing something fun. If he is out of town, then call an old friend or a family member you haven't seen in years and go see them. Take them to lunch and just talk. Enjoy yourself.

Sunday—Go to church and thank God for how good He has been to you. Then go home and rest. You will need it after the week you just had. Then on Monday, repeat the prescription.

Come back in two weeks for a follow-up appointment.

The woman was dumbfounded. She felt like an idiot. She had wasted her time going to this quack who had no idea what he was talking about. The more she thought about it, the more incensed she became. She felt like a fool! She swore she would *not* follow his silly prescription, and she poured herself a glass of wine that she sipped until she fell asleep on the couch while the television blared in the background.

A few days passed and she felt worse than ever. She thought about taking a cruise. She thought about redecorating the house. She considered flying to Paris for some shopping. Then she glanced down at the kitchen counter and saw the prescription. She realized it was Monday. In a moment of rage, just to prove the counselor wrong, she decided to do it! She got dressed and headed out the door, prescription in hand. She had nothing better to do.

Time passed. The counselor wondered what had ever happened to the rich old lady. She never called. She never came for her follow-up appointment. Then he eventually forgot about her—until about a year later when he ran into her in the grocery store. Literally.

He was rounding an aisle when a lady smashed into his grocery cart with hers. It nearly knocked his over. He looked up in disbelief, to see it was none other than the rich, depressed lady he had seen a year earlier. She recognized him at the same moment he recognized her. He spoke first.

"Well, hello there! I thought I would never hear from you again. You never came back for that follow-up visit. I guess you decided not to take your prescription."

She replied, "Oh, I am so sorry about that. I meant to call and then it just slipped my mind. I have had so much going on, and right now I'm trying to get all these groceries for our banquet tonight at the battered women's shelter. We've raised thousands of dollars and are having a banquet for the moms and the donors who are supporting the shelter. I would love to chat but I have to get these groceries and get back since I'm in charge. Thanks for the prescription!"

It worked. It still does. Though it is counterintuitive to all that we crave to satisfy our greed and selfish egos, when we act on the commands of Christ, that action kills our apathy. When we move according to the orders Christ has given us, that movement sets into motion the life-giving blood that pulses through our veins. We gain the muscle and endurance to run the race set before us (see Hebrews 12), and we leave behind the meaningless, selfish pursuits that depressed and discouraged us. We become servants of the most high God.

Jesus had some good insight into the human condition. When we live selfishly we eventually implode and die. But when we give our lives away in the service of God and others, life springs up all around us. This is what we were made for.

CHAPTER 16

Don't Lose the Muscle

Do you not know that in a race all the runners run,
but only one gets the prize? Run in such a way as to
get the prize. Everyone who competes goes into strict
training. They do it to get a crown that will not last; but
we do it to get a crown that will last forever. Therefore
I do not run like a man running aimlessly; I do not
fight like a man beating the air. No, I beat my body
and make it my slave so that after I have preached to
others, I myself will not be disqualified for the prize.

—1 CORINTHIANS 9:24-27

THERE ARE NO SHORTCUTS IN LIFE. In anything. Period. Even if you get rich quick by winning the lottery or something as unlikely as that, you won't keep it. You might get rich, but you won't stay rich. You can't lose weight unless you move more and eat less. You can't learn anything by cramming information in your head before a test. Success comes over time as we practice the little things with excellence and steadfastness.

We learn the deep things of God and see the truth in the paradoxes and mysteries of Scripture as we daily and faithfully exercise our faith through obedience. In doing this consistently, we build spiritual muscle that strengthens our weak hearts and minds.

The apostle Paul had seen some races in his day. Greek and Roman culture was obsessed with the human body and with competitions that pitted one person against another. He understood that training, movement, and discipline were necessary to win. Those who wound up victorious were willing to endure the pain for a greater prize.

Paul used this analogy for the Christian who intends to pursue a relationship with God. Without the pain of discipline there is never victory. We must move in obedience when God commands, or we will constantly face the defeat of hopelessness, discouragement, and apathy.

As a runner, I relearn this lesson every single time I stop running for any period of time longer than seven days. Running challenges my physical limitations. It forces my heart rate up. It opens my pores as sweat cleanses the toxins from my system. It toughens up my feet and makes them ache for hours after a good run. My hips hurt. My knees hurt. My lower back hurts.

But only for about a week.

After a week of running, my body adjusts to the stresses and strains. The aches slowly go away. I feel the ability to run farther and faster. The pain in my knees and hips diminishes and I can actually see the muscles in my legs developing. I sleep better at night. I am a more pleasant person to be around. I think more clearly and even my memory works better. Of course, science backs this up, pointing to chemicals with fancy names like adrenaline, endorphins, and dopamine. But what I know for a fact is that I feel better and am better when I am getting up and moving.

But eventually something changes. I hurt my shoulder in a basketball game. I have a three-week stretch of events that keep me away from home more than usual. It rains on the days I had planned to run. Or maybe we just hit a cold stretch in December and it's easier to stay inside and read a book or play checkers with my kids than to get up and put on my shoes and stretch. Whatever the reason, I find myself hitting these seasons where I just stop running. In the back of my mind I keep telling myself I need to get back outside on the pavement. And I keep telling myself that the longer I wait to hit the bricks, the longer it will take me to get back in shape and get my legs back under me. But things come up. Kids get sick and phone calls have to be returned, and before I know it, it has been four weeks since I logged any "foot time."

Then the dreaded day comes. The sun is shining, and I find myself with two hours before my next appointment. I could take a nap (because I am tired, which is a by-product of not running). I could work on another sermon. I could watch something we've recorded on DVR. Or I could suck it up and get outside, take the time to warm up and stretch and run.

I always end up running again. And it hurts. The longer I wait to run again the more it hurts. Just like the longer we wait to obey Christ by dying to ourselves and putting others first, the harder it is when we finally get there.

Then something really awesome happens. It happens every single time. The first mile is excruciating. I want to turn around and go home. Or just sit down at the side of the road and wait for someone to come pick me up and drive me home so I don't have to walk back. Nonetheless, I keep running. I push through the pain, and about the second mile, I get my second wind. I feel my lungs fill up with air and my heart rate stabilizes. Then a rush of energy floods my legs and lungs and the sweat begins to pour out of every pore on my upper body. I am back in the zone! I start feeling good again. I seriously consider making this little jog my own personal, official marathon. Twenty-six miles? Yeah, I got this.

Overcome with adrenaline and dopamine, I feel like I can run forever. But since it is my first time back in a few weeks, the good feeling is short-lived. At about mile four, the euphoria wears off. And I feel it in my legs first. They feel like they're planted in wet cement. They grow heavier with each step. As I churn and churn harder to move them, my lungs work harder to supply oxygen to the rest of my body. My breathing shortens and my heart rate spikes. I am paying the price for taking all that time off.

I limp home and stretch outside while the sweat still pours from my body. After a shower I feel a sense of accomplishment engulf me. It is that first day back that's the hardest. I know tomorrow will be easier. I tell myself that tomorrow, no matter what, I will run again. It is vitally essential that I make time for a run tomorrow. Sometimes I even say it out loud to myself as I slowly lower myself into bed, joints creaking and 200 mg of ibuprofen coursing through my dog-tired muscles.

When I take time off from running or exercising or working out, I lose the muscles I use when I'm committed to a regimen. It takes time to gain it back, but it always comes back. Without exception. Every single time. The process is painful, but the payoff is worth it. The muscles respond to action. They respond to vigorous movement. They are torn down at the fibrous level and they hurt, but then they repair themselves and recover as they re-attach stronger than before. The pain was good for me. The muscles are on their way back, and the lungs and the joints will follow.

☙

Just like a muscle loses its strength, our hearts lose the will to do the hard things Jesus demands of us once we slack off. A few Sundays pass by with you lying in bed instead of joining your community for corporate worship. Before long it has been a year since you've been in church. You let your tithe slip during a tight time financially and then you realize you've not given a dime to the work of the gospel or the local church in six months. I stop sharing my faith. I stop praying a prayer of humble thanks before a meal. You stop kneeling by your bed in prayer when you first wake up. And slowly…we lose the muscle. We begin living again like we are in charge. We place ourselves back in first place. The more we do what we want to without regard for the authority of Christ in our lives, the easier it is to slip comfortably into apathy and lethargy.

We must engage in movement and action if we are to gain back what we lost. So we get up and

> There is a payoff involved when we surrender our lives to the authority of Christ and place Him first, removing ourselves from the place of ultimate authority.

get moving. We often make the crucial mistake of thinking we'll wait until we *feel* like it. This is utter foolishness! I never *feel* like running. I never *feel* like eating healthy. I never *feel* like going to the gym. I never *feel* like brushing my teeth before bed when I am fatigued and ready for sleep. I never *feel* like drinking water (I would prefer coffee, sweet tea, or soda). But I do these things IN SPITE of how I *feel* because they are GOOD FOR ME. The future payoff is good health, joints that still move, low cholesterol, strong teeth that can chew soup without shattering, and a clear mind that's able to recall my best memories from childhood and adolescence when I am in my seventies.

There is a payoff involved when we surrender our lives to the authority of Christ and place Him first, removing ourselves from the place of ultimate authority. Actually, there are many. If we obey now and do the things that are right and good for us in spite of how we feel, we will one day see the wisdom of doing it God's way, of putting others first in light of the gospel. Here are a few of the long-term perks of being submitted to a life of radical discipleship.

We experience the very tangible presence of God on a regular basis.

We enjoy knowing that the God who made the universe is using us as part of His big plan to love humanity and redeem His creation.

We get to see His plan unfold with twists and turns and surprises we would never have dreamed up ourselves.

We gain the friendship and companionship of sisters and brothers who have also embraced God's paradox of finding life by losing it.

We occasionally see unexplainable, supernatural miracles take place, and then we get to tell those stories to people and watch their jaws drop.

We are delivered from the shallow, destructive, unhappy American pursuit of more and more junk. Stress levels and debt drop while joy levels and peace skyrocket.

We trust God for the results of our obedience and are delivered from the hellish life of "making things happen" by our own efforts.

We live in anticipation of God's ultimate redemption and return, when He will, in the words of N. T. Wright, "set all things to rights."

Let's not overcomplicate things here. We know the will of God by doing the will of God. And the will of God is not that hard. We trust Him for provision and protection. We submit our stubborn wills and desires to Him and exchange our death for His life. We obey the gospel by glorifying Him in how we live and by serving others in numerous and creative ways. We read the Bible and then we do what it says, by God's grace. And we do these things, ultimately, with a sense of certainty that He has the last word and the results are up to Him. We run the race not for a medal or a trophy. We run for the ultimate prize of gaining Jesus! He is our motivation, and our destiny, and the most valuable prize we could ever hope to attain.

So relax. Quit feeling bad for all the stuff you aren't doing for God, and just start moving toward Him. You will find yourself right smack dab in His presence when you obey His call to love your neighbor and love your God with all your heart. It starts now. Get up and start moving toward Him. If you don't, you will be disqualified from ever receiving the prize. Don't let apathy set in and make you sedentary. Keep moving toward the finish line and you will find Him waiting for you there.

CHAPTER 17

My Big Break

AMERICANS LOVE TO HEAR STORIES of the underdogs coming out on top. I admit that I too am a sucker for a rags-to-riches story where someone with amazing talent or ability rises from anonymity to fame and fortune because they can sing, act, or play a sport.

The Internet and *American Idol* have further ingrained this love affair with instant stardom into the collective subconscious of our society. Nameless nobodies are discovered and, right in front of an entire nation on a reality show, they overcome the odds and win. And to top it all off, sometimes we even feel a sense of pride in the matter because we got to vote for them!

It seems like everyone is looking for their big break. And if we can't get it ourselves, we live it out vicariously through the stars we create.

There was a point in my life, long before reality TV took over the world, that I too was looking for my big break. Although my call as a minister was about making much of Christ and little of me, I had easily forgotten that the backward life of a disciple is lived so that Jesus is the star, the hero, the main character—and I simply play a small role in support of the bigger mission.

I hit a stretch where I became ambitious to make a name for myself.

I wanted to be a sought-after speaker. I wasn't dying to live for the sake of the gospel. I was dying to become better known as an itinerant preacher.

In the summer of 2000, I received a last-minute phone call from a hopeful pastor that I thought would change the trajectory of my ministry forever. A very well-known Christian band, one of the top three in the country as a matter of fact, had just contacted this man and informed him they needed to play in his city in Kentucky on a Saturday night during their tour to fill a date that had been cancelled at the last minute. They were giving him a killer deal by dropping their fee to nearly nothing. He agreed to book and promote the concert, and then he called me to see if I would come and preach that night. He knew there would be a very big turnout because of the popularity of the band and the cheap ticket prices. He wanted someone to come preach the gospel and give an invitation since he knew the band didn't do that kind of thing. So I got the call.

My heart began to beat hard and I felt sweat begin to break out on my forehead. My first thought was a selfish one. Ironically, after walking with Jesus for over a decade, instead of being humbled at this chance to preach the gospel, I reacted in the opposite way.

I thought to myself, *This is the break I've been waiting for! These guys are the hottest thing going in the Christian world right now! And if I get to speak at their concert, maybe I'll get to meet them backstage. Maybe they'll hear me preach and love it! And if things go really well…they may even take me on tour with them, first as their road pastor, and then eventually as the tour speaker. Yes! Imagine that! Every night, in every major American city, the band takes the stage, blisters through a tight set, and then introduces ME! I walk out on the stage to the thunderous applause of thousands of fans who've never seen me before, but will love what they hear. And when the tour is over, I will have made a name for myself. I will be in high demand. People will know me, bands will want me on their tours, I will have to hire a major booking agent, and I will be set for life. This is my big break.*

I told the man yes. Of course I would come and speak for the event!

Isn't it odd how completely oblivious we are to our own selfishness and greed? When I look back now—even read the words in the above paragraph—I'm not sure what I'm most disgusted by—my pride and arrogance, or my stupidity at not seeing how pompous my motives were.

I called friends and sent e-mails and let everyone know I was speaking at this gigantic event with one of the most popular Christian bands of the day. All week during our Crossroads camp, I kept thinking about the concert, the crowd, the feeling of exhilaration when I would walk up the steps to preach, and meeting the band backstage. It never occurred to me that all my good feelings about this opportunity were revolving around *me*—

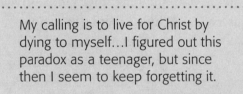

My calling is to live for Christ by dying to myself...I figured out this paradox as a teenager, but since then I seem to keep forgetting it.

how I would feel, what people would think of *me*, how people would love *my* sermon, and how this concert was going to catapult *me* to superstardom. From the way I was thinking, Billy Graham was going to meet me after my message and hand me the reins to his ministry.

What a silly sinner I was, and I didn't even realize it.

As a minister of the gospel, my calling is not just to preach and teach. My calling is to live for Christ by dying to myself. It is to love others by serving them, to find life by obeying the call to be dead to my sin and selfishness. I figured out this paradox as a teenager, but since then, I seem to keep forgetting it. But that's all right, because God keeps reminding me.

When the day finally arrived for my departure, I was like a kid who'd been waiting on a trip to Disney World. Even though I was totally fatigued from preaching at Crossroads for weeks on end, I found a boost of energy and excitement just from the adrenaline rush of knowing I would share the stage with a great band in front of thousands of people. So I boarded the flight that would take me to my big break.

I had a layover in Atlanta. It was July and it was hot. The concert was going to be in a high school gym. Someone was coming to pick me up from the airport at my final destination. I would spend the night and fly back the next day. This was going to be a piece of cake. Until I arrived at my gate in Atlanta and got the bad news. Our flight had been delayed, and our gate had been changed. All passengers had to report to a Delta service desk to be rerouted or re-ticketed. And then, over the intercom blared this announcement.

"Ladies and gentlemen, may I have your attention. If you were booked on the 12:05 flight to Nashville, please proceed to the Delta service desk for further information. That flight has been cancelled. It seems as if the aircraft is on fire."

True story. I glanced out the window to where the plane was parked and, sure enough, there was lots of smoke and flames coming from one of the engines. I was happy to take another flight.

So with about a hundred other people, I moved to the Delta service desk. We had to form a line, but since I fly so much, I have achieved Delta Silver Medallion status. Sounds fancy. And it is. I get special treatment. I get to board first. I get free upgrades. I get preferential treatment if flights are delayed or cancelled. And I get to move to the front of the line. Actually, any line. The only people above me on the food chain are Gold and Platinum Medallion fliers.

As the line began to form, I began to panic because I was toward the back. If I missed my connection I would miss my big shot at the big time. I had to get on that flight! The fate of *my* reputation, *my* name, *my* ministry, *my* future—everything—was on the line. So I debated for a few moments over whether to just wait where I was or move to the front of the line, flashing my fancy Silver Medallion card as I cut in front of the peasants. It was actually okay for me to cut according to the rules—no kidding—but I felt bad doing it. Then pragmatism won out. I could justify it because an entire city in Kentucky needed to hear me preach, and this was my big chance I could not risk missing out on.

I moved to the front of the line with only three people ahead of me. I was feeling very positive about my chances of making it in time for the concert. Then from nowhere a man appeared. Not just any man. A loud, obnoxious man with an accent. He was screaming into a cell phone at some unlucky listener. He was carrying an expensive leather briefcase. His suit looked tailor-made, and his shoes were just awesome. His wrist was decorated with a Rolex. He just oozed with importance. He was somebody. And he acted like he knew it. Completely oblivious to everyone else in the line, he proceeded to step directly in front of me. He looked at me absently. Then he turned his back to me. He never stopped talking on his phone. He continued to berate the person and give orders concerning a sale of some sort while my blood began to boil.

Just who in the world did this guy think he was? He couldn't just cut in line like that! We were all standing there before he arrived. And he didn't even say, "Excuse me" either. He wasn't from the South—that much was clear. He could have at least had the manners to say, "Pardon me." Never mind the fact that I had essentially just done the same thing based on my frequent-flier status. It's never convenient to confuse the facts with how I feel about something. Even though he could have been Gold or Platinum and had every right to break in front of me.

As I grew angrier at every word he barked into the cell phone, I decided to confront him. I was going to let him know how inappropriate it was for him to cut in front of a hundred other passengers. I would explain to him that there are rules of etiquette that need to be followed.

Deep in my heart, my selfishness was finding its way out, showing itself for what it really was. This was not about him. It was about *me*. I was on *my* way to *my* event, where people would hear *me* and I would be discovered as the next great Christian speaker. And if anything stood in *my* way, be it an airplane engulfed in smoke and flames or an annoying CEO with a thick New Jersey accent, I would stop at nothing to get what was *mine*.

So I reared back with my right arm. I placed my middle finger and trigger finger together for support. My aim was to poke him in the back of his shoulder hard enough to drill a hole through it. And when he turned to see what I wanted, I would unleash the fury of my wrath and embarrass him in front of all the other passengers waiting in line behind us. Again, it never dawned on me that I was supposed to be going to Kentucky to tell people about Jesus, the man who gave His life as a servant and calls us to do the same thing. I didn't even see the hypocrisy in the attitude of my heart at that moment, because I was intoxicated by the hope of making it big and was thinking that the concert I was headed to was the event that would get me there. The desire of my heart was evil, so it was easy to lash out at anyone who stood in my way.

Does this sound vaguely familiar to you at all?

As my arm was about to descend, fingers poised to drill into this man's shoulder blade, I heard a voice. I really do believe it was the Hoy Spirit. Here is my translation of what I heard.

So, Clayton King, gonna be a big-time speaker. Gonna head on up to Kentucky and impress the band tonight, huh? Well, I guess I see what you're really all about. You are about YOU. Not Me, or My gospel, or seeing people saved. All you want tonight is to be noticed. When you're on the stage preaching, you're really good at telling people how to live and act. But when you're off the stage, this is how you act. You better be careful.

I almost told the Holy Spirit to hush, but on second thought, I decided to listen and obey. I actually felt a sick feeling of conviction overtake me. In a momentary flood of revelation, He showed me that my motivation was all wrong and my heart's desire was selfish, not godly.

I didn't care one bit about seeing students saved or about proclaiming the gospel or about making Jesus famous. The *only* thing I cared about was *me*. I wanted the stage, the spotlight, and the attention. I had not even prayed for the people in attendance! My only thought was impressing the band and getting my foot in the door with them. All of these thoughts rushed in on me right there, standing in line.

In the meantime, my arm—which I had drawn back full-strength to drill through the shoulder of the pushy guy in a suit who had cut in front of me—had actually landed on his shoulder. It seemed as if the Holy Spirit had so successfully distracted me from my previous intention of giving the guy a piece of my mind that I forgot I had begun the motion toward his shoulder with my hand. Instead of drilling a hole through him full-force, my hand sort of lost steam on the approach and simply rested gently on his shoulder. I'm sure he wondered who I was and what in the world I was doing.

The man turned toward me, took his cell phone from his ear, and spoke to me in a shrill and irritated voice: "What?"

I realized I had been having a conversation with the Holy Spirit, completely oblivious to everything around me. I stared at him for a second and realized he was talking to me. I said, "Excuse me?"

He looked at me like I had two heads. "What do you want?"

"Why do you ask?" I replied.

"Because you have your hand on my shoulder!"

Embarrassed, I realized what was happening and tried to think of something to say that would alleviate some of the awkwardness of the moment I found myself locked into. It wasn't often I found myself with my hand draped casually upon the shoulder of a male stranger in a crowded airport.

My mind began to race. So I asked myself, *What is the one thing I can always do when I say something stupid or do something boneheaded— the one thing that's a guarantee to get me out of trouble? What works with my wife?*

I immediately knew what I had to do.

I said, "Sir, I just wanted to tell you…you look nice today. Have you lost weight?"

Total silence. Then a look of confusion followed by exasperation. With his cell phone still glued to his ear and deer-in-the-headlights look on his face, he blurted out, "Are you crazy?" And then the whole thing became an afterthought. He went back to screaming into his phone at the unlucky recipient on the other end, and I felt like I had avoided a verbal tongue-lashing I had provoked because of my pride.

I was congratulating myself, when someone behind me poked *me* in the shoulder. I turned to face a young man no more than 20 years old. His face was youthful and filled with exuberance.

"I know you get this all the time," he said, "but are you Clayton King, the speaker?"

My face got hot and my neck tightened up. "Yep, that's me." Conviction fell on me like firebombs from heaven. What was this guy going to say to me?

His words to me as I stood in line waiting on a flight disturbed me, even though they were meant to encourage me. He said, "My name is Mike, and I heard you speak at Clemson University several years ago. That was the night I became a Christian. God saved me from some pretty bad stuff. Then the next year you came back to Clemson and preached on missions. That night I felt like God wanted me to commit my life to reaching people who had never heard the gospel. So I surrendered to whatever He wanted for me and I'm on my way right now to Central America for my first mission trip! Man, I am so pumped! And I can't believe that I got to meet you finally, since you were the one who led me to Christ and preached the message that God used to call me to ministry. I look up to you so much and hope I can be the kind of man of God one day that you are. Isn't it cool that God sent you here today just for me, so I could meet you here in the airport?"

Wow. If he only knew. God didn't send me there to encourage *him*.

God sent him to speak to *me,* to convict me of my selfishness and re-mind me that people are always watching. If he only had known the thoughts that had consumed my mind just minutes before he recog-nized me, he could have lost all respect for me.

Now you can understand why this disturbed me. At that moment, I was *nothing* like a man of God. Just seconds earlier I'd been ready to unload on a guy for daring to step on my turf, daring to assume a place ahead of me in line, daring to disrespect *me,* the great Christian speaker! If I had not listened to the clear word of conviction that God spoke to my heart, the sin nature (the selfish, sin-ful, proud, and haughty pattern of living and thinking) would have raised its head up and made quite a scene. And if that had happened, the young man who was already watching me from just a few feet away could have had his vibrant and pure faith crushed through the horrible witness of a guy looking for his big break instead of living a life characterized by humility and the cross.

> It is God's rich mercy that continually kills that part of me that is ugly and greedy and selfish so that I can be filled with the measure of His fullness.

It makes me think once again of the words of Christ Himself. I still slip back into the mind-set of a Pharisee when I want to be first in line, or when I want to be seated at the head of the table, or when I want to exercise my rights and flex my spiritual muscles while parading my ministerial pedigree. How sick and contemptible! With as much mercy as I have been shown, you would think that by now I would have this thing practiced to perfection.

Alas, it just doesn't work like that. Even though I have been cru-cified with Christ and the old me is dead and there is a brand-new man alive in Jesus, somehow that old influence still lingers and lurks around our lives and makes appearances at inopportune times. These appearances serve to remind me that I must still, every moment of every day, rely on God's mercy. I must still, after decades of walking with Jesus, choose to daily die to my flesh and be made alive by the Holy Spirit living in me. I am still dying so I might live. And it is God's rich mercy that continually kills that part of me that is ugly and greedy and selfish so that I can be filled with the measure of His fullness.

When I finally arrived at the event, I did preach, and God did move. As a matter of fact, many teenagers and adults responded to the public invitation to repent of their sins and trust Christ. I rejoiced that I had the honor of proclaiming the gospel that evening. But I preached it with a little more humility after being reminded that just a few moments of fighting in my flesh for honor and position can do great damage to those watching my witness.

When you get the choice, choose to be last. Assume the attitude and position of a servant. And in doing so, you will be following the example of Jesus, our humble Savior. In the long run this means much more than the temporary benefits of being first.

CHAPTER 18

Life from Death: Paul Prassad

*I eagerly expect and hope that I will in no way be ashamed,
but will have sufficient courage so that now as always
Christ will be exalted in my body, whether by life or by
death. For to me, to live is Christ and to die is gain.*

—Philippians 1:20-21

THERE IS NO PLACE ON EARTH LIKE INDIA.

I have been there seven times and each trip has had a different and distinct impact on my life. But the event that left the deepest impression on me from all my time spent there was meeting Paul Prassad. I've never met anyone who has ever embodied in such fullness the idea of dying to live or the paradox of finding life by losing it. I tell his story in the hope that you will see Christ more clearly and surrender to His lordship in a new and fresh way.

I met Paul on a trip in 1997. Like Thomas in John 11, this humble pastor was willing to go with Jesus wherever He led him, even if it cost him his life. He was willing to follow Jesus and die with Jesus, and I had never encountered such a man.

⚜

Paul Prassad was a pastor in a large city in India and boldly proclaimed the gospel among his people, nearly all of whom were Hindu. And just as every religion has its zealots, so does Hinduism.

Because Paul was leading Hindus to faith in Christ, he began to draw attention to himself. But the real reason he was making waves was that he was baptizing converts. In much of the world, baptism is considered the moment where everything changes, where the old life and even the old religion dies. In Muslim and Hindu culture, a new convert to Christ is often declared dead by their family. Occasionally a mock funeral will be held. They lose all rights of inheritance. It's not uncommon to hear of Christian converts being beaten publicly for humiliating their family by abandoning the faith of their ancestors and embracing Christianity (the religion of the West and the United States). Often it is the family of a new convert that causes them the most pain and suffering once they put their trust in Jesus.

Paul Prassad was preaching the gospel effectively because not only were Hindus repenting of their sins, they were also getting baptized. And this was the final step in a total conversion to Christianity. Though every Hindu I have ever met was kind and peace-loving, nothing gets the radical Hindu zealots worked up like seeing people baptized. Nothing.

This humble pastor caused such a stir that a small group of dedicated zealots made the decision to shut him down. They arrived at his church one Sunday morning to warn him, as a courtesy, that he was no longer welcome in their city. They expected him to close down his church and leave. They were going to beat him in the street if he did not leave immediately. Paul decided to preach the message he had prepared and as a result, he was dragged into the road after church and assaulted by these men who wanted him to take his Christianity and his church somewhere else. He was bruised and bloodied and warned, "Do not return next Sunday or we will be waiting for you to kill you."

But when you really love something, or someone, it is no sacrifice at all to suffer for that love. I feel this way about my own family and would do absolutely anything to assure their safety and health.

True disciples, radical disciples, will lose it all for the One who gave it all for them.

Paul Prassad felt this way about Jesus. He had dedicated his life to preaching the gospel and nothing could stop him. The beating hurt. The threats were frightening. But they didn't eclipse the compelling power that was at work in him to declare the love of Christ in a city filled with lost souls. He would return the next Sunday. His life, and his death, belonged to Jesus.

Next Sunday came. They met him outside the small building in the city where his church met and once again reminded him of the fate that awaited him if he chose to preach the gospel again. He told them, in simple words, that they could do whatever they wanted to him, but he had committed to die as a martyr for Jesus and was ready if his time had come.

The men waited in the back until the service concluded. They then proceeded to drag Paul outside the building into the street again. This time they beat him so badly that they broke bones. While a growing audience gathered, no one attempted to rescue him for fear of the fate that would await them, the same fate he was suffering. With another warning not to return, the men left him broken in the street.

I admit this would most likely have been enough for me had I been the beaten pastor. I would have taken this as a sign from God that He was calling me to plant a church in another city, and I would have put my house on the market while sending out resumes. But Paul Prassad, like the disciple Thomas, understood on a deeper level that some things are worth dying for. Jesus was most definitely worth it. In being persecuted for Christ, we feel the suffering of Christ as we suffer with Christ.

The next Sunday was horrific. The same angry men met Paul, quickly reminded him of why they were there, and waited for the service to end. Again they dragged him into the street but with more conviction this time. What happened next was simply awful.

They stripped him naked to embarrass and shame him, an unthinkable experience for anyone in Indian culture but particularly for a man. Then they opened his mouth and poured battery acid down his throat. While several men held him down, another man pummeled him in the stomach to make him swallow the acid. The flesh inside his mouth, his gums, his throat and esophagus, were all scorched and burned raw.

Then they took a long metal rod with a razor-sharp pointed end. And without going into detail, by the time they were finished with Pastor Paul, he was lying on the street with his intestines beside him, on the ground, outside of his body. They had disemboweled this man simply for proclaiming the gospel. They left him lying in his own blood and waste, certain he would die in a matter of moments.

How he survived can only be due to a miracle of God and the toughness and tenacity of someone who has been captured by the grace of the gospel—changed to such a degree that the option of dying is simply not on the table, because it would mean leaving unfinished the work of preaching the love of God to those who need it most. Somehow, Paul survived. Most of his intestines were removed and a colostomy bag was attached to his side so he could eliminate waste.

Of course, the next Sunday, a week after he was left for dead in the street, he returned to preach to his congregation.

Word had gotten out that he was alive, and the angry mob of men was there. Partly to finish the job once and for all, and partly to see if the rumors were true—and if they were, to try to decipher why, exactly, this man kept coming to his own lynching. This was particularly odd, considering all he had to do was go to another town to preach. But he just kept coming back.

Paul hobbled into the building, anticipating certain death after his message and the baptism he had planned at the end. Knowing this would be his final message, he preached on loving your enemies and forgiving those who do evil to you. He wanted to leave his parishioners with the commands of Christ to not return evil for evil, and he

wanted his death to be a testimony to the saving grace
of God's forgiveness. None
of the saints who gathered
there that day ever expected
to see their pastor alive after the service. His enemies

> In mid-sentence, Paul
> was interrupted…by one
> of his assailants from the
> previous week, who was
> sitting in the back.

had proven their resolve. Paul had proven his. Now it was time for the
showdown, and it seemed as if evil would win.

The men met Paul as he entered. They told him they would finish
the job if he insisted on preaching. He did, and they followed him inside the building and stood in the back waiting. Waiting for the end.
The end of the sermon and the end of their enemy.

The message did not go as planned. In mid-sentence, Paul was interrupted. He was interrupted by one of his assailants from the previous week, who was sitting in the back, evidently waiting for the service
to end so he could kill Paul. This man stood to his feet and began to
scream. The words, however, were not filled with malice and threats.
The man begged Paul to stop preaching.

"Please stop! I must ask you to stop right now! I cannot suffer
through this anymore. I must meet Him. I must ask Jesus to save me,
and to forgive me for all my evil deeds! You say we should forgive our
enemies. And I am your enemy. And the horrible things I have done
to you are haunting me and I need to be forgiven for them. I want
Jesus to forgive me! I want to become a Christian! I want to do it here
and now! I denounce all other gods, and I want to be forgiven by Jesus
Christ and baptized!"

The man walked forward in utter brokenness, and Paul was able to
embrace one of the very people who just a week earlier had forced him
to death's door. They stood weeping and praying together as the Hindu
became a Christian. He had received forgiveness.

The only way a human being can react the way Paul reacted is if

Jesus Christ has transformed them at a deep level. Paul Prassad understands dying to live. His tormentor was so moved and undone by the fact that this pastor could preach on forgiving your enemies just one week after he was nearly killed that he forsook his heritage and family and religion and converted to faith in Christ.

This kind of Christianity is convicting and contagious. I pray that many more people would embrace dying to live as their way of life, and that Paul Prassad would be an example of what God can do with a life totally surrendered.

CHAPTER 19

Take Up Your Cross

HOW DO I WRAP UP A BOOK about giving your life away first to God, then to others? What could I say that would resonate within your heart and mind and leave an impression that won't be forgotten once the book is finished and closed and placed on your shelf?

The best thing to do is go right back to where we started. The words of Jesus launched us into a journey of discovering life by dying to sin and selfishness. We will continue that journey by God's grace.

But perhaps the most troubling thing Jesus had to say about dying to live dealt with the actual way He would die and His expectation of us as a result of how He died. Let me begin this way…

More Than a Slogan

In marriage, I have learned many things, but one lesson continues to surface regularly. I constantly misunderstand things my wife says to me. She means one thing as a woman, but as a man I hear something different. I presume a majority of married couples face this challenge even after decades of life together.

Christians are not that different. When we misunderstand the meaning of what Jesus said, we often reduce the great depths and mysteries of Scripture to cute clichés that fit on our T-shirts or bumper

155

stickers, and we minimize the hard sayings of Christ by reducing them to Christian slogans. Sometimes these slogans catch the attention of a seeker or an unbeliever, but I fear they most often communicate not only our shallow understanding of the gospel, but our laziness in trying to show the world that God loves them.

Among our most treasured and often repeated Christian slogans is this familiar four-word statement made by Jesus, recorded in Mark 8. It's a catchy phrase sandwiched in between a scathing rebuke and a reminder of the cost of following Jesus.

Take up your cross.

This phrase has now been employed to describe everything from getting your wisdom teeth pulled to being mocked for going to church on Sunday mornings instead of to the golf course. And while our application of these four simple words can be as varied as the daily difficulties we attach them to, we may need to pause for a minute and stop asking what "take up your cross" means to us today…and instead ask what it meant to the people who actually heard Jesus call them to do it. Once we see more clearly what it meant to them, we can more correctly apply it in our own lives. The phrase did mean something very specific to the audience that gathered around Jesus. Let's explore it together.

Thomas (the doubter, and the one who was ready to die with Jesus in John 11) was almost certainly there the day Jesus found Himself reminding the growing crowd that followed Him exactly why He came to earth after all. And what Thomas, Peter, the rest of the disciples, and the throngs of hungry Jewish people heard from the Lord was exactly opposite of what they wanted. They heard Jesus tell them that if they wanted to live, they had to die.

The stage is set in Mark 8 for Jesus to work up the gigantic following to an even greater level of excitement. His teachings had struck a chord with the common people. His message was easily interpreted by Jewish peasants as a call from God to rise up against Roman tyranny, purge the Holy Land of all pagan powers, and restore the glory of the ancient kingdom of David. For decades the Romans had occupied Israel. Their soldiers filled the streets to keep the peace. Their tax collectors levied unbearable tax burdens on Jewish citizens to pay for the occupation. The Jews hated their oppressors and loathed their culture. And to top it all off, the Romans were Gentiles who did not worship God or follow any Jewish religious or cultural rules. All of Israel prayed for the day when God would send a Messiah to topple the foreigners and remove the scourge from Jerusalem. The crowds who followed Christ assumed He was that Messiah.

Adding to the insult of Roman occupation was the rule of Herod, the Roman puppet king who was a genius at public works and building amazing structures (the Herodium, a palace, and a massive system of aqueducts are two examples), as well as a demented madman who murdered anyone suspected of insurrection or betrayal (including his own family members). In an attempt to keep the peace of Rome in Israel and placate the Jewish religious establishment, he had a magnificent temple rebuilt on the existing foundation. This pleased those who saw Rome as a protective power but angered Jewish nationalists, who saw Rome as the wicked enemy to be expelled.

It is no wonder Jesus found such a following among His own people when He arrived on the scene! Not only did He heal the sick (who could not afford a doctor) and feed the hungry (who had no money to eat adequately because of their heavy Roman tax burden), but He also preached about the kingdom of God and its imminence. The Jewish people went crazy. Jesus had to be the Messiah, because He could cast out demons and perform other miracles. And surely He was the military Messiah who would get rid of the Romans once and for all!

This sounds a lot like me. I have my own misunderstandings of Jesus, and those ideas I impose on Him serve my own personal agenda. I want a Jesus who will help my finances and keep me healthy. I want a Jesus who gives great benefits but demands little responsibility. I have my own idea of what Jesus is supposed to do for me. And that perspective must die. So it was with the crowd in Mark 8.

Evidently, Jesus looked at the throngs of people following His every move, and knew He had to remind them He was not their kind of Messiah. He did not come to kill, but to die. He did not come to be served like Herod or Caesar, but to serve and to save. And He wanted His disciples to practice what He modeled for them. So He spoke a few simple words packed with dynamite.

> *If anyone come after me, he must deny himself and take up his cross and follow me. For whoever wants to save his life will lose it, but whoever loses his life for me and for the gospel will save it* (Mark 8:34-35).

What did this mean?

It was a loaded phrase, to be sure. Peter had already rebuked Jesus for saying He was going to die. Peter had his own agenda for Jesus, much like the rest of the Jews who had put their hope in Jesus' power to remove Rome. And when Jesus told them He must die, Peter saw all of his dreams vaporize. If Jesus died, then so did the revolution and the movement against Rome. It had gained too much momentum to let it stop now!

But Jesus wouldn't be intimidated or distracted from His mission, no matter what ideas His followers had about what He should do or how He should lead. He was God. He was on a mission. He would not be detoured or deterred.

And to emphasize this to His followers, Jesus used a phrase that was utterly despicable, revolting to a Jewish audience. He picked the most offensive and disgusting reference of the day, one that would have immediately drawn the minds and memories of everyone there to an event filled with bloodshed, suffering, and death.

Take up your cross.

We know where this phrase comes from by studying other historical writings from this time period. We even find a passing comment in the Scriptures that sheds some light on what it meant. In Acts 6, Gamaliel, a Jewish leader, makes a passing reference to Judas the Galilean, who evidently led a revolt of Jewish Zealots against the Romans (all in the context of a discussion by the Jewish Council on how to punish Peter and others for preaching the gospel):

> *After him, Judas the Galilean appeared in the days of the census and led a band of people in revolt. He too was killed, and all his followers were scattered* (Acts 5:37).

With a bit of research, it becomes clear that this particular uprising was one of the most bloody in Jewish history. It seems that Judas had gathered hundreds, maybe even thousands (depending on which historian you read) of men by capitalizing on their hatred of the Romans and had convinced them he was the Messiah. He told them that if they followed him, he would lead a rebellion straight into the heart of Jerusalem that would rid the Holy Land of all Gentile power. They would be his conquering army. And they did march into Jerusalem, but they were quickly cut down by the highly trained and battle-hardened Roman soldiers. Hundreds were killed in this bloodbath, but in order to make an example of them, the Romans decided on a more brutal form of punishment.

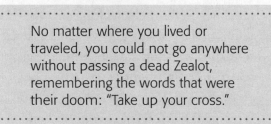

No matter where you lived or traveled, you could not go anywhere without passing a dead Zealot, remembering the words that were their doom: "Take up your cross."

The surviving Zealots were each led up to a cross, the Romans' favored form of execution, and on the busiest streets and intersections of Jerusalem, they were told by the Roman soldiers, "Take up your cross." Each rebel was forced to drag his cross along the streets and marketplaces in full view of every Jewish man, woman, and child until the soldiers told them, "Lay down your cross." And then, on the spot where he laid down his cross, he was crucified upon it.

The Zealots hung on those crosses for days until they died of suffocation, or blood loss, or wounds sustained in battle. But as a final blow to the failed rebellion, the Romans would not allow their families to take their bodies down after they died. If you were caught attempting to remove the body of a dead Jewish Zealot, you could be hung on a cross beside them. It was Rome's way of further crushing the spirit of a nation that had allowed a rebellion to arise. It was a genius move to use this as a reminder of how Rome dealt with rebels.

The city was filled with the stench of hundreds of rotting human corpses for weeks. And no matter where you lived or traveled, you could not go anywhere without passing a dead zealot, remembering the words that were their doom: "Take up your cross." It was nothing new for Rome to crucify its enemies. But in Jerusalem they left their enemies on those crosses long after they were dead. For years, the skeletons of the zealots clung with lifeless tenacity to those wooden crosses, bleached white by the sun, reminding every passerby of the price that was paid in an attempt to gain freedom.

What would you have done if your father had been caught and crucified? What if it was your husband or brother or son? Would you have stayed by their side as they hung there dying? Would you have attempted to help them and risked your own life? Could I have watched as they heaved and jerked upon crosses from the spasms of pain that racked every muscle? Would I have been able to stand the screams and pleas for help? And what would I have done after their death?

Could we have ever walked by their crosses—knowing their bones still hung upon them? Imagine living for 20 years in Jerusalem and knowing exactly where your brother's remains were hanging, and dealing with the emotional devastation of never being able to lay his remains to rest in the ground? This was a diabolical form of punishment not just for those who were crucified but even more so for those who loved them, mourned their death, and were forced to live on in the shadow of those crosses.

Now think about Jesus addressing the crowd in Mark 8. Can you imagine the emotional tension and upset and horror in the crowd as Jesus called the people to die to themselves? The memories of seeing those men up on those crosses were still fresh and raw, even though it had happened decades earlier. And historians tell us that even up to a hundred years after this rebellion, skeletons still hung upon crosses along the roads of Palestine.

Rome got what it wanted. A slaughter of insurrectionists. A shame and a deterrent to any Jews who might ever dream of another rebellion. And a long-lasting tangible reminder, hung on crosses that lined the streets, of what happened to those who took up arms against the empire.

It would not surprise me to eventually find out, perhaps in heaven, that Jesus spoke these radical words in full view of one of those very crosses, with a Jewish rebel's bones still hanging from it. Can you just imagine the kind of impact the phrase "take up your cross" would have had on those listening if Jesus had spoken those words while standing directly in front of, or underneath, a cross with the remains of a skeleton still clinging to it after years of exposure to the sun and the elements?

Why in the world did Jesus choose these words? To endear his disciples to Himself, to motivate people into faith and fidelity to His mission? To weed out those who were following Him to see the next trick, the next miracle, the next show of power? To get rid of those who were waiting for the next free meal? Or to send a message out to the masses who had their bellies filled and their minds blown by His power and authority that He had not come to destroy the Roman Empire but to destroy death, evil, sin, and selfishness by what awaited Him on a cross, just like the ones that lined the roads of Jerusalem?

Simply put, He was telling the truth. He was preparing those who would choose to follow Him that they would be called upon to die in order to live.

The truth just sounds different. It compels people in a different way than the slickest sales pitch. Jesus calls out to the heart of the matter and to our hearts, and He bids us come and die so we gain everlasting, abundant life in knowing Him.

> *This is eternal life: that they may know you, the only true God, and Jesus Christ, whom you have sent* (John 17:3).

Dying to ourselves means dying to what we want, because we almost always want something that benefits us and, by default, hurts others. But when we take up our cross, it means we deny ourselves and thus place Christ into the center of all we are and all we do. It is a daily dying—one that is never fully completed but is in constant motion. It is as if the corpse of sin keeps coming back to life, demanding to be fed and cared for. But by the cross, we learn a most important lesson from a perfect example.

Consider what Jesus did for you on the cross and think about these words from Timothy Keller:

> If the beauty of what Jesus did moves you, that is the first step toward getting out of your own self-centeredness and fear into a trust relationship with him. When Jesus died for you he was, as it were, inviting you into the dance. He invites you to begin centering everything in your life on him, even as he has given himself for you.[13]

Jesus showed us through His death and sacrifice what dying to live really meant. He died so we could live. If you read this book and miss that most central and most important point, then not only have you wasted your time, but you are wasting your life by living it apart from knowing Christ.

This world and this life are not about us. We are but small parts of a bigger story. God's story continues to unfold, and the main character is Jesus Christ. We play very small supporting roles, and God gives those to us. We do not pick and choose them.

All of this is made possible through the cross. It is our joy to live by its power as it compels us to find life by losing it. God's paradox continues to call us toward death, and by following that call, we find life.

CHAPTER 20

Parting Shot

How I HAVE RELISHED the honor of writing for you in hope that you would see the beauty and necessity of living life like Jesus did—putting others first, for the glory of God, as His handcrafted masterpiece.

And if you know me at all, and perhaps you do, then you know I almost never conclude a messsage without extending an invitation from God to the listener, or in this case, the reader. Every good sermon always ends with two words: Will you?

Will you embrace all that God did for you in Jesus?

Will you extend your hands and receive His grace and forgiveness?

Will you live in response to His example and find your life by giving it totally to Christ in worship and obedience?

Will you die so you can live?

This is the question that still calls out for an answer, all the way from Calvary—from the hill they called Golgotha, from a bloody, splintered cross. Will you come and die? Will you follow Jesus?

> The question is then posed to us in the strongest and clearest possible way: Dare we stand in front of the cross and admit

that it was all done for us? Dare we take all the meanings of the word GOD and allow them to be recentered upon—redefined by—this man, this moment, this death?[14]

If you dare look at what Jesus did for you, how can you resist surrendering absolute control of your life to Him? If He is stirring your heart right now, if you feel Him moving you, if what you have read resonates in your soul and you know you were born to die to your sins so that you could find life by giving it totally to Jesus, then do it. Give your life to Him. Right now. Speak to Him, call on Him for help and rescue, confess your sins to Him and repent. Be forgiven and cleansed and set free from the misery of being in charge of your own life. Ask Him to save you and tell Him that you want Him to be in charge. You will know something has changed eternally. You will know you have just been made alive. For the very first time.

Resources for Further Exploration

Celebration of Discipline by Richard Foster. HarperCollins, San Francisco, 1998.

The Cost of Discipleship by Dietrich Bonhoeffer. Simon and Schuster, New York, 1995.

Death by Love by Mark Driscoll and Gerry Breshears. Crossway Books, Wheaton, IL, 2008.

Evil and the Justice of God by N.T. Wright. InterVarsity Press, Downers Grove, IL, 2006.

Jesus and Empire by Richard A. Horsley. Fortress Press, Minneapolis, 2003.

Mere Christianity by C.S. Lewis. Collier Books, New York, 1960.

Peace with God by Billy Graham. W Publishing Group, Nashville, 1984.

The Reason for God by Timothy Keller. Dutton Books, New York, 2008.

The Valley of Vision by Arthur Bennett. The Banner of Truth Trust, Carlisle, PA, 1975.

Vintage Jesus by Mark Driscoll and Gerry Breshears. Crossway Books, Wheaton, IL, 2007.

Why a Suffering World Makes Sense by Chris Tiegreen. Baker Books, Grand Rapids, MI, 2006.

Wishful Thinking by Frederick Buechner. Harper and Row Publishers, New York, 1973.

Notes

1. Billy Graham, *Peace with God* (Nashville, TN: W Publishing Group, 1984), pp. 110-111.

2. Taken from *The Valley of Vision: A Collection of Puritan Prayers and Devotions,* ed. Arthur Bennett (Edinburgh, Scotland: The Banner of Truth Trust, © 1975). Available from www.banneroftruth.org.

3. C.S. Lewis, *Mere Christianity* (New York: Collier Books, 1960), p. 46.

4. Richard Horsley, *Jesus and Empire* (Minneapolis, MN: Fortress Press, 2003), p. 126.

5. Dietrich Bonhoeffer, *The Cost of Discipleship* (New York: Simon & Schuster, 1995), p. 44.

6. Bonhoeffer, p. 45.

7. Richard Foster, *Celebration of Discipline* (San Francisco: Harper Collins, 1998), p. 9.

8. Mark Driscoll and Gerry Breshears, *Death by Love* (Wheaton, IL: Crossway Books, 2008), p. 201.

9. Bonhoeffer, p. 94.

10. Chris Tiegreen, *Why a Suffering World Makes Sense* (Grand Rapids, MI: Baker Books, 2006), p. 62.

11. Tiegreen, p. 62.

12. *USA Today,* Tuesday, April 14, 2009.

13. Timothy Keller, *The Reason for God* (New York: Dutton, 2008), p. 221.

14. N.T. Wright, *Evil and the Justice of God* (Downers Grove, IL: InterVarsity, 2006), p. 100.

A WORD FROM CLAYTON ABOUT CROSSROADS WORLDWIDE

In 1995, I began a nonprofit ministry out of my college dorm room called Crossroads. It began with my preaching ministry and now includes multiple layers of ministry that stretch all around the world.

- *Summer camps.* Several thousand middle- and high-school students come from all over the United States every summer to our Crossroads summer camps, where they hear teaching and preaching from God's Word and participate in group activities, sports tournaments, corporate worship, and community missions.

- *Student conferences.* Every January during Martin Luther King Jr. weekend, we host a three-day conference for middle- and high-school students, as well as a separate conference for college students and young adults.

- *Mission trips.* We send short-term volunteer teams to India, Malaysia, Haiti, the Navajo reservation in Arizona, and various other places to share the gospel. We also support a full-time volunteer couple in the Himalayas as they assist in running a Christian hospital.

- *Community discipleship home.* We host two intensive discipleship programs for people ages 18 to 25, one in Boiling Springs, NC (a 12-month program) and one in Manali, North India (a 6-month program).

- *Preaching ministry.* I travel full-time, teaching and preaching on evangelism, discipleship, missions, and relationships. I speak at conferences, colleges, churches, retreats, concerts, and public schools. I began this ministry at age 14 and have preached in 45 states and 30 countries to over 2 million people.

- *Writing.* In addition to the five books I have written, I consistently write about issues that face Christians, pastors, leaders, parents, and spouses on my blog at ww.claytonking.com.

- *Media.* I have dozens of audio and video sermons online for free. Find them at

www.claytonking.com
www.newspring.cc
www.liberty.edu
iTunes: "clayton king live" or "clayton king"

For more information or to schedule one of our speakers, contact us at
www.crossroadsworldwide.com
crossroadsworldwide@gmail.com
704-434-2920

O₂
Breathing New Life into Faith
Richard Dahlstrom

Your physical body needs balance in breathing. Inhale, exhale…one leads naturally to the other. The same rhythm is essential in the life of faith. You inhale life-giving strength from God through things like prayer, study, solitude, and silence. You exhale generosity, hospitality, and service to the poor. If you try to do one without the other, you won't last very long. This fresh perspective on the classic disciplines of the faith will empower you to process the oxygen of the Spirit.

SEX, FOOD, AND GOD
Breaking Free from Temptations, Compulsions, and Addictions
David Eckman

The good things created by God, like food and sex, can be misused to run away from emotional/relational pain. When this happens, the damage and loneliness can wreck your life. David Eckman shows how and why unhealthy appetites trap people in a fantasy world, and how shame and guilt—and the addiction cycle—are broken when we realize how much God delights in us.

101 FREQUENTLY ASKED QUESTIONS ABOUT HOMOSEXUALITY
What Causes Same-Sex Attraction? Can a Christian Be Gay? Is Change Possible for a Homosexual?
Mike Haley

- Our pastor says that all homosexuals are going to hell. Is he right?
- I've heard that 10 percent of the population is homosexual. Is this true?
- I think someone I know is struggling with homosexuality. How do I approach him without pushing him away?

Here are answers to the biggest FAQs on homosexuality, fielded by an expert on the subject and a former homosexual, Focus on the Family's Mike Haley. Mike gives straightforward responses to help you, whether you're personally impacted by homosexuality or just want to know more.

THE GOD QUESTION
An Invitation to a Life of Meaning
J.P. Moreland

True happiness comes not from seeking pleasure but from a deep sense of meaning and purpose. So…maybe it's time to give authentic Christianity a fair hearing.

"Becoming an apprentice of Jesus in the school of life," as the author calls it, will get you down to the essential questions about a life of faith:

- How can anyone really know God exists?
- Seriously, is an intimate relationship with God actually possible?
- What does a twenty-first-century disciple of Jesus look like?

Here you can honestly explore an entirely new way of living—the way of Jesus.

DATING WITH PURE PASSION
More than Rules, More than Courtship, More than a Formula
Rob Eagar

Is there more to true love than you've been told? Rob Eagar shares the forgotten, Christ-centered answer. *Dating with Pure Passion* shows you how to break the cycle of empty relationships and find healthy potential partners—and how to appreciate sexual desire and also resist temptation. Most important, you'll begin to understand how God is working *for* you in the relationship issues you face.

> "Dating with Pure Passion *is a great resource for anyone seeking God's design in lasting relationships.*"
>
> **LOUIE GIGLIO**
> Founder of Passion Conferences

GRACE WALK
What You've Always Wanted in the Christian Life
Steve McVey

Nothing you have ever done, nothing you could ever do, will match the amazing joy of letting Jesus Christ live His life through you. It is the only way to experience a passionate Christianity. As you connect with His love and friendship, He will do more *through you* and *in you* than you could ever do for Him or for yourself. Today is the day to start walking the grace walk.

To learn more about other Harvest House books
or to read sample chapters, log on to our website:

www.harvesthousepublishers.com

HARVEST HOUSE PUBLISHERS
EUGENE, OREGON